EYE TO I
3,000 Years of Portraits

October 27, 2013 to February 16, 2014
Katonah Museum of Art

Funding for this exhibition was provided by ArtsWestchester, with support from Westchester County Government; the New York State Council on the Arts with the support of Governor Andrew Cuomo and the New York State Legislature; and the Museum's Exhibition Patrons. Additional sponsorship provided by Janet Benton, Karen B. Cohen Foundation, Judy and Tony Evnin, Betty Himmel, Alexia and Jerry Jurschak, Kendal on Hudson, KMA Docent Supporters, Victoria and Stephen Morris, Yvonne and Leslie Pollack, and Lisbeth and Frank Stern.

Foreword

How does an exhibition engage the viewer? This is a critical question for museums, and the Katonah Museum of Art is eager to make its exhibitions more relevant and interactive. To this end, we have taken an idea from a show we mounted in 1990 titled *Do You See What I See?* In this earlier collaboration with the Hood Museum at Dartmouth College, we asked professors from various departments to explore works of art through the prisms of their own academic disciplines. We then involved our audience by inviting them to submit their thoughts on cards collected in cigar boxes.

For our current exhibition, *Eye to I...3,000 Years of Portraits*, we are again seeking individual responses and have traded index cards for touchscreens. Many more community members have been engaged at the outset—art collectors, artists, businesspeople, educators, musicians, poets, politicians, scholars, and other local individuals—who have contributed original commentary for the catalogue. Reading through these pages, accessing technology in the galleries, and visiting our ever-changing exhibition website eyetoi.org, you will see that these responses have invited new interpretations.

This concept, that each viewer comes to art with his or her own experiences, education, memories, and DNA is, perhaps, an obvious truism. We are privileged to take this even further, not only through technology, but also through the groundbreaking scientific research of Eric Kandel, Nobel Laureate, neurobiologist, and founding director of the Center for Neurobiology and Behavior at the College of Physicians and Surgeons of Columbia University. *The Age of Insight*, Dr. Kandel's most recent book, explores the interconnections between science and art through psychology, brain science, and research into how the brain processes visual information. His focus on the viewer's active, creative participation—the beholder's share—as well as research findings that show "faces are by far the most important category of object recognition" are particularly relevant for this exhibition. We are proud to be part of the dialogue and invite you, too, to join the conversation.

Acknowledgments are due to the many individuals who have participated in this multi-layered exhibition from concept to completion.

Nancy Hitchcock, Ellen Keiter, and Yvonne Pollack are to be thanked for their dedicated efforts as co-curators and exhibition organizers. Nancy Wallach and Neil Watson also made valuable contributions.

Numerous individuals and institutions graciously loaned artworks. Many are local community members. We are thrilled to present such a fine and varied collection of portraits. Similarly, we are grateful to the writers who shared their insightful, inspiring, and sometimes humorous responses to the works of art. Their voices define the spirit of *Eye to I*.

Several generous sponsors have made this exhibition possible: Janet Benton, Karen B. Cohen Foundation, Judy and Tony Evnin, Betty Himmel, Alexia and Jerry Jurschak, Kendal on Hudson, KMA Docent Supporters, Victoria and Stephen Morris, Yvonne and Leslie Pollack, Lisbeth and Frank Stern, ArtsWestchester, New York State Council on the Arts, and the Museum's Exhibition Patrons.

As always, our hardworking staff and volunteers invested time and much energy in this project. Naomi Leiseroff and Aura Fraiman Lewis are responsible for the expert execution and creative catalogue design. Lisa Harmon was a talented editor. Nancy Hitchcock managed all loans and worked with our skilled installation crew to bring Dean Ebben's exhibition design to life. Rachel Actis, Diana Knoblauch, and Yvonne Pollack led superb docent training sessions. Margaret Adasko, Pam Hart, Karen Stein, Helena Vidal, and Ellen Williams created a wide variety of innovative educational offerings, including a new model for thematic docent tours. Jessica DeRosa and Margaret Moulton developed compelling and enjoyable special events and public programs. Sarah Marshall and the Marketing Committee designed and implemented a clever marketing campaign celebrating the exhibition's many faces. Camila Engelbert was the perfect partner to help us forge a new path with interactive technology in the galleries.

It is with much gratitude that we recognize the loyal support of the Museum's Board of Trustees, Overseers, and volunteers.

Belinda Roth
Interim Executive Director

Introduction

Do you see what I see? Probably not. *Eye to I ... 3,000 Years of Portraits* stirs the debate with a provocative and interactive approach to viewing art.

Eye to I represents diverse cultures and spans more than thirty centuries of history and art. The exhibition is not intended as an encyclopedic account of portraiture; rather, it uses portraits to explore the myriad ways that individuals look at and understand imagery. The conceptual framework for this show is based on the premise that no two people respond to an artwork in the same way. The importance assigned to an object corresponds to viewers' perspectives, which vary according to language, culture, socialization, education, and other aspects of their personal histories. The portrait genre in particular presents multiple layers of interpretation and represents a broad sampling of cultures, media, and diverse artistic approaches.

Our definition of portraiture is an inclusive one. We present literal representations of historic individuals, idealized faces signifying social or ethnic identity, and abstract constructs that don't contain a face at all. There are portraits made in commemoration or as a commission, others that serve political or religious purposes, and those that explore the psychological realm of the self and others. We have taken an intentionally expansive view of what constitutes a portrait.

Each of the 65 artworks is accompanied by interpretive copy from a variety of individuals. Over 120 contributors—from a U.S. poet laureate to a local police chief—share their personal responses to the portraits on display. Visitors are encouraged to contribute their own observations on video touchscreens and iPads, as well as on their home computers We hope this dialogue will be ongoing and engaging, both in the galleries and in cyberspace.

There are no experts here. The range of responses reflects the diversity of our community. Our views of an artwork were transformed with each new submission. We were continually amazed by the varied and creative ways people chose to engage with the art. You may refer to the *Did You Know?* section in the back for curatorial information modeled on traditional museum label copy. We intentionally omitted this text from the illustrated pages—it is the viewer's voice we value.

We are grateful to the many individuals who took time to look, reflect, and share their observations with us and our visitors. We are also thankful to the numerous private collectors, many of them local, who agreed to lend their cherished artworks for the public to enjoy.

We dedicate this catalogue to our audience.

**Nancy Hitchcock, Ellen Keiter, and Yvonne Pollack
Co-organizers**

Face to Face With Portraiture

By Eric R. Kandel

Portraits. The Katonah Museum of Art could not have selected a more fascinating topic from the perspective of brain science. There is a magic to portraits—of all we respond to in the world, faces are the most special.

As Charles Darwin first pointed out in his book *The Expression of the Emotions in Man and Animals*, faces are essential for social interaction. We recognize each other and even ourselves through our faces. Moreover, as social animals, we need to communicate not only our ideas and plans, but also our emotions to one another. Facial expressions are our primary social signaling system. They are central to all social communication, from forming a friendship, to making a business arrangement, to finding a partner.

Darwin proposed that we convey our emotions in large part through a limited number of facial expressions—about seven of them (Fig. 1). Thus you can attract another person by smiling seductively or you can repel that person by looking foreboding.

Since faces have the same number of features—one nose, two eyes, and one mouth—the sensory and motor aspects of emotional signals communicated by the face must be universal, regardless of culture. Darwin argued that both the ability to form facial expressions and the ability to read the facial expressions of others are innate, not learned. Years later, experiments in cognitive psychology showed that face recognition does indeed begin in infancy. From birth onward, infants are much more likely to look at faces than at other objects. In addition, infants have a predilection for imitating facial expressions, a finding that is consistent with the central role that face perception plays in social interaction.

It is therefore of particular interest that our brain treats faces differently from all other objects. Computers that can solve complex mathematical and logical problems have great difficulty with face recognition, yet the human brain is extraordinarily good at it. Moreover, we can readily recognize a line drawing of

a face; in fact, a slight exaggeration of facial features makes it even easier for us to recognize a person. One reason for this is that our brain processes faces in unusual ways, as we shall see.

Thirty Centuries of Portraiture

Prehistoric art contains very few examples of human portraiture. Some of the first representational art is thought to be the 17,300-year-old paintings on the walls of the Lascaux Caves in southwestern France. Human beings appear very rarely in them, and they are never central. Leaving behind a visual record of one's life or of others was not uppermost in the minds of prehistoric people. Rather, the earliest cave paintings represent animals, fierce animals.

Portraiture comes from a different lineage and has played a key role in Western art. For centuries before the advent of photography, affluent and influential families used portraits to convey power and status as well as to show descendants what their forebearers looked like.

Beginning around 15,000 BC, Egyptians used portraiture to depict their godlike rulers, the pharaohs. These images were painted and carved in places of spiritual importance and they were used to show not only the appearance, but also the power and symbolic significance that their leaders held. The Greeks of the early 7th century BC also undertook portraiture, mostly in the form of sculpture, but their portraits represented people of power and influence as well as gods—believing that artistic depiction conferred godlike status. This tradition was continued in Rome in the 1st century BC. Portraiture declined in the Middle Ages, however, when the only portraits were religious depictions.

In the transition from the Middle Ages to the Renaissance, the portrait began to be used as a stand-in for the living person, representing the subject when he or she was absent. In this role, portraits converted transience into permanence, conjuring a self that would outlive death. The task of a great artist was to ennoble his subject by depicting the sitter's

  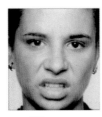   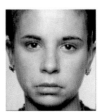 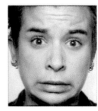

| Happiness | Surprise | Disgust | Contempt | Anger | Sadness | Fear |

Figure 1
The valence of facial expressions of emotion, from happiness (inviting approach) to fear (inviting avoidance).

lasting significance. This was done most commonly by painting subjects in profile.

Portraiture in the Renaissance depicted the noble and affluent, presenting not only their physical and psychological appearances and their characters, but also expensive objects and luxurious surroundings. Until the 16th century, royalty and rulers were the typical subjects, but as the economy shifted wealth to the merchant class, portraiture also shifted from profile paintings to head-on renderings. This change is sometimes referred to as the "Renaissance gaze shift." Renaissance artists favored the direct gaze, which allows the subject to make eye contact with the beholder and to convey enduring character traits.

The method of painting also changed. In the Renaissance, paintings were made with egg tempera, a mixture of egg yolk and powdered pigment that gave rise to colorful works of art containing high contrast, a medium not available to medieval painters. In Holland, Jan van Eyck used an even newer medium—oil-based paint—that made possible an even greater range of color, and therefore increased contrast and depth. Later, in the 17th century, in addition to their revolutionary new oil paints, the Dutch painters Rembrandt and Franz Hals, and the Italian sculptor Bernini, introduced the play of emotion on the human face to a degree that had not been present in earlier works, such as those by Raphael or Titian.

Portraiture was initially successful because viewers could compare the portrait in front of them with their memory of the subject, whom they knew to be a person of stature and accomplishment. Modern artists changed that. Their subjects could be commoners or aristocrats. Moreover, their subject no longer necessarily represented all members of his or her class, but was portrayed as an individual.

Since Rembrandt and the Dutch School of the 17th century, artists have tried to get below the surface appearances of their subjects. Over a century earlier, Raphael had described a portrait by the 15th-century painter Fillipino Lippi as being more like the sitter than the sitter himself (Scharf, 1935). In other words, for a portrait to be a work of art, it must not simply resemble the sitter. As the French sculptor Auguste Rodin said, "If the artist only reproduces superficial features, as photography does, if he copies the lineaments of faces exactly, without reference to character, he deserves no admiration. The resemblance which he ought to obtain is that of the soul." Vincent van Gogh expressed a similar sentiment when he said, "Ah! Portraiture, portraiture with the thought, the soul of the model in it. That is what I think must come." And finally, Alice Neel said, "Like Chekov, I am a collector of souls. I think if I hadn't been an artist I could have been a psychiatrist."

The portraits of the Austrian modernists carried this psychological tradition into the 20th century—the Age of Insight. Gustav Klimt, Oskar Kokoschka,

and Egon Schiele succeeded brilliantly in revealing their subjects' inner lives. They did this by mastering the perceptual principles that guide our eyes and brain in constructing the psychological world around us. Klimt's intuitive grasp of the power of implied line, contour, and the viewer's experience enabled him to create some of the most subtle and sensual drawings in all of modern art. The key creative achievement of Kokoschka's and Schiele's expressionist portraits was to engage our innate capacity for understanding other people's minds and emotions. The artists' intuitive comprehension and careful study of how faces, bodies, and hands communicate emotion and solicit empathy enabled them to convey dramatic new psychological insights. In parallel with Sigmund Freud, they knew how to enter the private theater of another's mind, to understand its nature, mood, and emotion, and to convey that understanding to the viewer.

The Beholder's Share: The Beginning of a Scientific Approach to Portraiture and Art

The idea of relating portraiture to science came from Alois Riegl. He and his disciples at the Vienna School of Art History, Ernst Kris and Ernst Gombrich, attained international renown at the end of the 19th century for their efforts to establish art history as a scientific discipline by grounding it in psychology and sociology.

Riegl revealed a new psychological aspect of art: namely, that art is

incomplete without the perceptual and emotional involvement of the viewer. Not only does the viewer collaborate with the artist in transforming a two-dimensional likeness on a canvas into a three-dimensional depiction of the visual world, the viewer interprets what he or she sees on the canvas in personal terms, thereby adding meaning to the picture. Riegl called this phenomenon the "beholder's involvement" (Gombrich later elaborated on this concept and referred to it as the "beholder's share"). Based on ideas derived from Riegl and contemporaneous schools of psychology and psychoanalysis, Kris and Gombrich devised a new approach to the mysteries of visual perception and incorporated that approach into art criticism.

Kris studied ambiguity in visual perception and those studies led him to elaborate on Riegl's insight that the viewer completes a work of art. Kris argued that every powerful image is inherently ambiguous because it arises from the experiences and conflicts of the artist's life. The viewer responds to this ambiguity in terms of his or her own experiences. The extent of the viewer's contribution depends on the degree of ambiguity in the image.

The idea of ambiguity as Kris used it was introduced by the literary critic William Empson, who held that ambiguity exists when "alternative views [of a work of art] might be taken without sheer misreading." Empson implied that ambiguity allows the viewer to read the aesthetic choice, or conflict, that exists within the artist's mind, whereas Kris held that ambiguity enables the artist to transmit his sense of conflict and complexity to the viewer's brain.

The Problem of Perception

Gombrich extended Kris's ideas about ambiguity to visual perception *per se*. In the process, he came to understand a crucial principle of brain function: our brain is not simply a camera, it is a creativity machine. It takes incomplete information from the outside world and makes it complete.

Any image projected onto the retina of the eye has countless possible interpretations. Therefore, as Gombrich realized (1960), visual perception is only an important piece of a larger question that Western philosophy has long debated: How can the real world of physical objects be known through our senses? The Anglo-Irish philosopher George Berkeley, Bishop of Cloyne, had already grasped the central problem of vision as early as 1709, when he wrote that we do not see material objects *per se*, but the light reflected off them (Berkeley, 1709). This light then passes through our eye's lens and onto our retina, the flat layer of light-sensitive tissue lining the eye's inner surface. As a result, the two-dimensional image projected onto our retina can never directly specify all three dimensions of an object. This fact, and the difficulty it raises for understanding our perception of any image, is referred to as the inverse optics problem (Albright, 2013; Purves, 2010).

As Berkeley pointed out, the inverse optics problem arises because any given image projected onto the retina can be generated by objects of different sizes, with different physical orientations, and at different distances from the observer. For example, a souvenir model of the Eiffel Tower held close to the eye may appear identical in shape and size to the actual Eiffel Tower as seen from across the Champ de Mars. As a result, the actual source of any three-dimensional object is inherently uncertain. Gombrich fully appreciated this problem and cited Berkeley's observation that "the world as we see it is a construct slowly built up by every one of us in years of experimentation" (1960). Shortly after Berkeley's writings, David Hume and Immanuel Kant generalized this argument from vision to all perception. They argued that the real world is inevitability remote from us and that we can only appreciate it indirectly.

Edward Adelson (1993) and subsequently Dale Purves (2010), two contemporary students of vision who have revisited the inverse optics problem, ask how we are able to respond so successfully to the real world if our perceptions are illusory constructs. The answer is that our visual system must have evolved primarily to solve this fundamental problem. Even though there is not enough information in the image for our eyes to reconstruct an object accurately, we do it all the time. How?

An answer to this question was set forth by the noted 19th-century physician and physicist Hermann von Helmholtz, who argued that we solve the inverse optics problem by including two additional sources of information: bottom-up and top-down information (see also Adelson, 1993).

Bottom-up information is supplied by computations that are inherent in the circuitry of our brain and in the connections among cells that enable us to extract key elements of images in the physical world, such as contours and junctions. These computations are governed by innate, universal rules that are built into our brains by evolution. This is why, despite countless ambiguities, even young children can interpret images.

Top-down information is supplied by learning from earlier experience, from remembrance, and from the associations we bring to bear on every image we encounter, including a work of art. Thus, perception also incorporates knowledge based on learning, hypothesis testing, and goals—knowledge that is not innate. Because much of the sensory information that we receive through our eyes can be interpreted in a variety of ways, we must use inference to resolve this ambiguity. When, for example, we see a person growing larger and larger, we typically conclude that he or she is not rapidly expanding, but merely walking toward us. While we tend to draw such conclusions automatically, our brains must do some experience-based guesswork that is not based on the visual stimulus alone. We must guess, based on experience, what is the most likely image in front of us.

Helmholtz's remarkable insight is not restricted to perception: top-down processing applies to emotion and empathy as well. The noted cognitive psychologist Chris Frith of the Wellcome Center for Neuroimaging at University College London has summarized Helmholtz's insight: "We do not have direct access to the physical world. It may feel as if we have direct access, but this is an illusion created by our brain."

The influence of top-down processing on the beholder's perception convinced Gombrich that there is no such thing as an "innocent eye." All visual perception is based on classifying concepts and interpreting visual information. We cannot perceive that which we cannot classify, he argued. These insights inspired him to explore the psychology of perception more deeply than any art historian before him.

Riegl, Kris, and Gombrich realized that each of us brings to a work of art our memories, in addition to our bottom-up, built-in visual processes. We remember other works of art that we have seen. We remember scenes and people that have meaning to us. And when we look at a work of art, we relate it to those memories. In a sense, to see what is actually painted on a canvas, we have to know beforehand what we might see in a painting. In this way the artist's modeling of physical and psychic reality parallels the intrinsically creative operations of the brain in everyday life.

These psychological insights into perception were to serve

as a solid footing for a bridge between the visual perception of art and the field of biology.

The Brain as a Creativity Machine

As Gombrich's fascination with visual perception deepened, he became intrigued by Kris's ideas about ambiguity in art and began to study the ambiguous figures and illusions made famous by Gestalt psychologists. Simple illusions allow for two distinctly different readings of an image. Such illusions are uncomplicated examples of the nature of ambiguity, which Kris held was the key to all great works of art and to the beholder's response to great art. Other illusions contain ambiguous images that can lure the brain into making perceptual errors. Gestalt psychologists used these errors to explore the cognitive aspects of visual perception. In the process, they deduced several principles of the brain's

perceptual organization before neuroscientists discovered them.

Ambiguous figures and illusions intrigued Gombrich because he knew that in viewing a portrait or a scene, multiple choices are possible to the viewer. Often, several ambiguities are embedded in a great work of art and each of them may present the beholder with a number of different decisions. Gombrich was particularly interested in ambiguous figures and illusions that cause perception to flip between two rival interpretations.

One such figure is the drawing of a duck-rabbit (Fig. 2) created in 1892 by the American psychologist Joseph Jastrow and used by Gombrich in his book *Art and Illusion*. The viewer cannot see both animals at the same time. If we focus on the two horizontal bands at the left that look like a beak, we see the image of the duck; if we focus on the right, we see the rabbit, and the two bands at the left become long ears. We

can initiate the switch between rabbit and duck with a movement of our eyes, but that eye movement is not essential for the switch.

What impressed Gombrich about this drawing was that the visual information on the page does not change. What changes is our interpretation of the data. We see the ambiguous image and unconsciously infer, based on our expectations and past experiences, that the image is a rabbit or a duck. This is the top-down process of hypothesis testing that Helmholtz described. Once we have formed a hypothesis about the image, it not only explains the visual data, it also excludes alternatives. The image is no longer ambiguous. It is either a duck or a rabbit, but never both. This principle, Gombrich realized, underlies all of our perceptions of the world. Interpretation is inherent in visual perception itself; the two are not separate processes.

The Rubin vase (Fig. 3), devised by the Danish psychologist Edgar Rubin in 1920, while also an example of perception flipping between two rival interpretations, relies on unconscious inferences made by the brain. Unlike the duck-rabbit illusion, the Rubin vase requires the brain to construct an image by differentiating an object (figure) from the background (ground). The Rubin vase also requires that the brain assign "ownership" of the outline, or contour that separates the figure from the ground. Thus, when our brain assigns ownership of the contour to the vase, we see the vase, and when it assigns ownership to the faces, we see

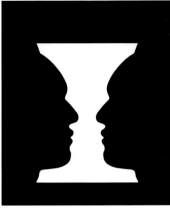

Figure 3
The Rubin vase

the faces. The reason the illusion works, according to Rubin, is that the contours of the vase match the contours of the faces, thus forcing us to select one image or the other.

Kris's and Gombrich's studies of ambiguity and of the beholder's share led them to conclude that the brain generates internal representations of what we see in the world around us, whether as an artist or a beholder. Moreover, they held that we are all wired to be "psychologists" because our brains also generate internal representations of other people's minds—their perceptions, motives, drives, and emotions. These ideas contributed greatly to the emergence of a modern cognitive psychology of art.

But Kris and Gombrich realized that their ideas were based on sophisticated insights and inferences; they could not be examined directly and therefore could not be analyzed objectively. To examine these internal representations directly—to peer into the brain—cognitive psychology had to join forces with brain biology.

Figure 2
The duck-rabbit

The Beholder's Share of Face Recognition: Psychology and Biology

As we look at a portrait, our brains are busy analyzing facial contours, forming a representation of the face, analyzing the body's motion, forming a representation of the body, experiencing empathy, and forming a theory of the person's mind. These are all components of the beholder's share, and modern biology makes it possible for us to begin to explore them. Figure 4 shows my initial approximation of the neural circuit involved in the beholder's share. It indicates seven points of analysis along the circuit and the areas of the brain involved in each.

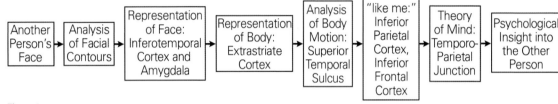

Figure 4
Flow diagram of the neural circuit involved in the beholder's share

Analysis of facial contours and the brain's representation of a face in a portrait are clearly of central importance to the beholder's share. Fortunately, we have learned a great deal about the psychology of face recognition and the biological processes underlying it.

Figure 5
Inverted images of Leonardo da Vinci's *Mona Lisa*
Adapted from Thomas, P., 1980. "Margaret Thatcher: a new illusion." *Perception*, 9: 483-484. p.483 Fig. 1.

Figure 6
Upright images of Leonardo da Vinci's *Mona Lisa*
Adapted from Thomas, P. 1980. "Margaret Thatcher: a new illusion." *Perception*, 9: 483-484. p.483 Fig. 2.

The Psychological Analysis of Face Recognition

Our brains are specialized to deal with faces. Indeed, face perception has evolved to occupy more space in our brain than any other figural representation. As Darwin pointed out, the face and the emotion it conveys are key to all human interactions. We judge whether we trust people or are scared of them in part by the facial expressions they show us. We are attracted to people, of the same sex and the opposite sex, because of their physical appearances and facial expressions.

Although face recognition is a difficult task for computers, we can recognize hundreds of faces effortlessly. We do even better when we see them in cartoon form, because our brains respond powerfully to exaggeration. Kris and Gombrich argued that the facial exaggeration used by the Mannerist painters, by cartoonists, and later by the Viennese expressionists is successful because our brains respond specifically to facial exaggeration.

The brain treats faces very differently from other objects. For one thing, face recognition is uniquely sensitive to inversion. If we were to turn a bottle of water upside down, we would still recognize it as a bottle of water. However, we might not recognize a face when it is upside down. Not only do we have difficulty recognizing an inverted face, we cannot under most circumstances recognize a change in expression on an inverted face. If we view two images of the *Mona Lisa* upside down (Fig. 5), we may recognize both of them as the *Mona Lisa* but not realize that they have different expressions. One is the enigmatic *Mona Lisa*; the other has a smirk on her face that we don't see until the image is upright (Fig. 6). With an object other than a face, we would see the difference.

The Representation of Faces in the Brain

Scientists learned an enormous amount about the representation of faces in the brain from people who have face blindness, or prosopagnosia. The condition, first described in 1947 by Joachim Bodamer, results from damage to the inferior temporal cortex, whether acquired or congenital. About 10 percent of people have a modest degree of face blindness. People with damage in the front of the inferior temporal cortex can recognize a face as a face but cannot tell whose it is. People with damage to the back of the inferior temporal cortex cannot see a face at all. In Oliver Sacks's famous story *The Man Who Mistook His Wife for a Hat*, a man with face blindness tried to pick up his wife's head and put it on his head because he misread it as his hat.

Chuck Close, one of the great painters of our time, struggles to handle three-dimensional forms. He cannot look at a face and deal with its complexity. This is because he suffers from prosopagnosia. Eventually, Close learned that he could recognize faces in his mind's eye if he flattened the three-dimensional images of a face into two dimensions. Using this ingenious method of coping with prosopagnosia, Close has spent his entire career painting nothing but faces; indeed, his whole artistic endeavor emerged in response to his inability to see the visual world as other people see it. Paradoxically, people with prosopagnosia can recognize inverted faces more easily than people without face blindness. This fact suggests that our brain contains an area that is specialized for upright face recognition.

Charles Gross at Princeton, and later Margaret Livingston, Doris Tsao, and Winrich Freiwald at Harvard, have made several important discoveries about how our brains analyze faces. Using a combination of brain imaging and electrical recording of signals from individual cells, they found six small structures, which they called face patches, in the temporal lobe of macaque monkeys that light up in response to a face. When the scientists recorded electrical signals from cells in these face patches, they found that different patches respond to different aspects of the face: head-on view, side view, and so on. They also found a similar, although smaller set of face patches in the human brain.

Studies by Tsao and a colleague (2009) have shown that the monkey's face patches contain a high proportion of neurons that respond only to faces. These cells are sensitive to changes in position, size, and direction of the gaze of the face, as well as to the shape of various parts of the face.

Figure 7 shows a cell in a monkey's face patch responding to various images. Not surprisingly, the cell fires very nicely when the monkey is shown a picture of another monkey (a). The cell fires even more dramatically in response to a cartoon face (b): monkeys, like people, respond more powerfully to cartoons than to real objects because the features in a cartoon are exaggerated. But the cell in the monkey's face patch follows Gestalt principles: a face has to be complete in order to elicit a response. When the monkey is shown two eyes in a circle (c), there is no response. A mouth and no eyes elicits no response (d). Two eyes and a mouth—a nose is not necessary—inside a square, also no response (e). If shown only a circle, no response (f). The cell responds only to two eyes and a mouth inside a circle (g). If the circles and the mouth are only outlined, there is no longer a response (h). In addition, if the monkey is shown an inverted face, it does not respond.

These studies have shed new light on the nature of the templates the brain uses to detect faces. Behavioral studies further suggest that there is a powerful link between the brain's face detection machinery and the areas that control attention, which may account for why faces and portraiture are such strong draws.

The Beholder's Share of Body, Movement, Empathy, and Theory of Mind

Our brain creates representations not only of faces, but also of bodies, and these are part of the beholder's share as well. Behind the visual cortex is an area called

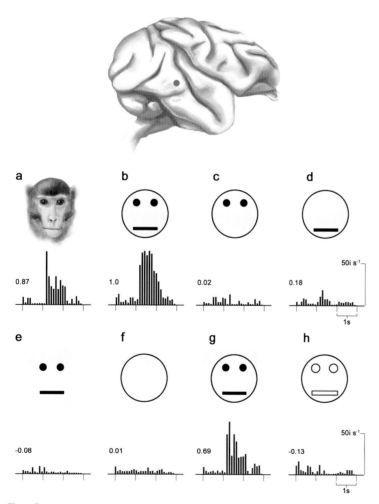

Figure 7
Using a visual stimulus to excite a single cell in a macaque face patch
Adapted from Kobatake, E., Tanaka, K. 1994. "Neuronal selectivities to complex object features in the ventral visual pathway of the macaque cerebral cortex." *J. Neurophysiol.* 71 (3):856-2280. p.859 Fig. 4.

the extrastriate cortex, which responds to body parts such as arms, hands, and legs. Behind that is an area concerned not just with the body but also with the processing of motion—all kinds of motion, artificial as well as biological. Another area analyzes just biological motion, such as an arm reaching forward or legs in motion.

Two additional areas in the brain—in the supplementary motor system—make up the mirror neuron system. Studies of monkeys have shown that mirror neurons respond when one monkey watches another monkey move: for example, when the observed monkey picks up a glass of water and drinks it. But these cells also respond when a monkey observes a person pick up a glass of water and drink it. These cells in the monkey's brain mirror movement.

This shows us that simply by observing movements we are training our motor systems to carry out those acts. Babies do this; we now think that they acquire some aspects of language by actually reading their parents' lips and quietly simulating their mouth movements, in addition to listening to them.

We know now that one of the reasons the modernist portraiture of Klimt, Kokoschka, and Schiele appeals to us so strongly is that our remarkably large, social brain contains extended representations of faces, hands, and movement, visual features that play prominent roles in the artwork of the Austrian modernists. We are hardwired

to respond to exaggerated depictions of facial features and bodies. Moreover, the brain's mirror neuron system, its theory-of-mind system, and its biological modulators of emotion and empathy endow us with a great capacity for understanding other people's minds and emotions.

Theory of mind is the idea that someone else has a mind of his or her own, with separate feelings, aspirations, and thoughts. For example, when you look at a painting of someone walking toward you, you may feel an urge to move and walk toward the person. When you look at a portrait of a person who is really interesting, you have empathy for that person; you try to understand what is going on in his or her mind. Theory of mind also enables us to predict what other people will do. It is a very important skill and our brain's temporo-parietal junction is devoted to it.

The New Dialogue Between Science and Art

Ever since Socrates and Plato speculated on the nature of the human mind, serious thinkers have sought to understand the self and human behavior. For past generations, that quest was restricted to the intellectual and often non-empirical frameworks of philosophy and psychology. Today, however, brain scientists are attempting to translate abstract philosophical and psychological questions about mind into the empirical language of cognitive psychology and brain biology. The guiding principle of brain

scientists is that mind is a set of operations carried out by the brain, an astonishingly complex computational device that constructs our perception of the external world, fixes our attention, and controls our actions. One of the aspirations of this new science of mind is to gain a deeper understanding of ourselves—including how we respond to, and create, works of art—by linking the biology of mind to other areas of humanistic knowledge such as fine art.

Establishing a dialogue between science and art is not easy, however, and it requires special circumstances. One such set of circumstances arose in 1900s Vienna, which I describe in my recent book, *The Age of Insight*. At the turn of the 20th century, Vienna was a relatively small city that provided a social context— the university, coffeehouses, and salons—in which scientists and artists could readily exchange ideas. Their dialogue was conducted in a common language derived from scientific medicine, psychology and psychoanalysis, and art history. That dialogue continued to develop in the 1930s, with the contributions of cognitive psychology and the Gestalt psychology of visual perception. This bold and successful advance provided the impetus for applying the insights of cognitive psychology to the biological study of perception, emotion, empathy, and creativity, thus leading to the new dialogue under way today.

Important insights into mind have come from writers and poets as

well as from artists, psychologists, and scientists. Each kind of creative endeavor has made and continues to make specific contributions to our full conception of mind. If we disregard one in favor of another, our understanding will be incomplete. After all, it took a psychologist like Freud to explain what unconscious processes are, but artists like Shakespeare, Beethoven, and the Austrian modernists to show us how some of those unconscious processes feel.

Scientific analysis represents a move toward greater objectivity, toward a closer description of the actual nature of things. This is accomplished in the case of visual art by describing the observer's view of an object not in terms of the subjective impressions the object makes on the senses, but in terms of the brain's specific responses to the object. Art, including portraiture, is best understood as a distillation of pure experience. As such, it provides an excellent and desirable complement to, and enrichment of, the science of mind. Neither approach alone is sufficient to understand fully the dynamics of human experience. What we require is a third way, a set of explanatory bridges across the chasm between art and science. How, then, do we extend the search for common concepts and meaningful dialogues? One way is to examine successful attempts and see how they were accomplished. How long did they take? How completely were they realized?

We can see how the unification of one field can positively affect others in the interaction of physics with chemistry, and of both with biology. In the 1930s Linus Pauling demonstrated that the physical principles of quantum mechanics explain how atoms behave in chemical reactions. Stimulated in part by Pauling, chemistry and biology began to converge in 1953 with the discovery of the molecular structure of DNA by James Watson and Francis Crick. Armed with this structure, molecular biology unified in a brilliant way the previously separate disciplines of biochemistry, genetics, immunology, development, cell biology, cancer biology, and more recently, molecular neurobiology. This unification has set a precedent for other disciplines. It holds out the hope that in the fullness of time, large-scale theories will include the science of mind.

In the case of art, these discussions might involve a modern equivalent of the famous salons in Europe, in which artists, art historians, psychologists, and brain scientists exchanged ideas with one another—only today the settings would be new interdisciplinary centers at universities. Much as the modern science of mind emerged from discussions between cognitive psychologists and brain scientists, now modern students of the science of mind can engage in dialogue with artists and art historians. It is quite likely that a new conversation between the visual arts and the science of perception and emotion will

continue to enlighten both fields, and that in time those cross-disciplinary exchanges may well have cumulative effects.

What benefits would this dialogue confer?

The potential benefits for the new science of mind are obvious. One of its goals is to understand how the brain responds to works of art, how we process unconscious and conscious perception, emotion, and empathy. But what is the potential usefulness of this dialogue for artists?

Since the beginning of modern experimental science in the 15th and 16th centuries, artists from Filippo Brunelleschi and Masaccio, to Albrecht Dürer and Pieter Bruegel, to Richard Serra and Damien Hirst have been interested in science. Much as Leonardo da Vinci used his knowledge of human anatomy to depict the human form in a more compelling and accurate manner, so, too, contemporary artists may use our understanding of the biology of perception and of emotional and empathic response to create new art forms and other expressions of creativity.

Today, for the first time, we are in a position to address directly what neuroscientists can learn from the experiments of artists and what artists and beholders can learn from neuroscience about artistic creativity, ambiguity, and the perceptual and emotional responses of the viewer. We have seen in this essay specific instances of how the art of portraiture and science can enrich

each other. Moreover, we have seen the potential of the new biology of mind as an intellectual force, a font of knowledge that is likely to bring about new connections between the natural sciences and the humanities. This could help us understand better the mechanisms in the brain that make creativity possible, whether in art, the sciences, or the humanities, and open a new dimension in intellectual history.

Eric R. Kandel, a professor of brain science at Columbia University, a senior investigator at the Howard Hughes Medical Institute, and a recipient of the 2000 Nobel Prize in Physiology or Medicine, is the author of "The Age of Insight: The Quest to Understand the Unconscious in Art, Mind and Brain, From Vienna 1900 to the Present."

References

This essay is based on *The Age of Insight: The Quest to Understand the Unconscious in Art, Mind, and Brain From Vienna 1900 to the Present*, New York: Random House, 2012, and I rely particularly on chapters 8, 14, 15, 16, 17, and 18, and the references therein. I also draw on material discussed in *Principles of Neural Science*, 5th ed., edited by Kandel, Eric R., Jessell, Thomas M., Schwartz, James H., Siegelbaum, Steven A., and Hudspeth, A. J., New York, McGraw Hill, 2013.

The essay draws further on a number of historical and contemporary sources:

Adelson, Edward H. 1993. "Perceptual Organization and the Judgment of Brightness." *Science*, 262:2042-2043. Oxford: Clarendon Press.

Albright, Thomas. 2012. "TNS: Perception and the Beholder's Share". *The Science Network*. Albright talk with Roger Bingham.

Albright, Thomas. 2013. "On the Perception of Probable Things: Neural Substrate of Associative Memory, Imagery, and Perception." *Neuron*, 74(2):227-45.

Belting, Hans, 2001, *An Anthropology of Images: Picture, Medium, Body*. Princeton and Oxford: Princeton University Press.

Berenson, Bernard. 1930. *The Italian Painters of the Renaissance*.

Berkeley, George. 1709. "An Essay Towards a New Theory of Vision." In *The Works of George Berkeley, Bishop of Cloyne*, edited by Arthur A. Luce and Thomas E. Jessop, vol. 1, 171-239. London: Nelson, 1948-1957. Originally published in George Berkeley, *An Essay Towards a New Theory of Vision*. Dublin: M Rhames for R Gunne.

Cummings, Laura. 2009. *A Face to the World: On Self-Portraits*. Harper Press: New York, NY.

de Costa, Esther and Wasserman, Fred, eds. 2003. *Schoenberg, Kandinsky, and the Blue Rider*. The Jewish Museum, Scala Publishers: New York.

Da Vinci, Leonardo. 1989. *Leonardo on Painting: An Anthology of Writings by Leonardo da Vinci with a Selection of Documents Relating to His Career*. Martin Kemp ed. Translated by Margaret Walker. New Haven, CT: Yale University Press.

Darwin, Charles. 1859. *On the Origin of Species by Means of Natural Selection, or the Preservation of Favoured Races in the Struggle for Life*. 6th edition. London: John and Murray. Accessed June 17, 2013. http://darwin-online.org.uk/content/frameset?itemID=F391&viewtype=text&pageseq=1

Freud, Sigmund. 1916. *Leonardo da Vinci: A Memory of His Childhood*, translated by Alan Tyson. London: Routledge and Kegan Paul, 1957. Originally published in Sigmund Freud, *Leonardo da Vinci*, translated by Abraham Brill. New York: Moffat, Yard.

Freud, Sigmund. 1955. "The Moses of Michelangelo." In *The Standard Edition of the Complete Psychological Works of Sigmund Freud*, edited and translated by James Strachey, vol. 8, 211-236. London: The Hogarth Press and the Institute for Psychoanalysis. Originally published in 1914.

Freiwald, Winrich and Tsao, Doris. 2009. "A face feature space in the macaque temporal lobe." *Nature Neuroscience*, 12:1187 – 1196.

Frith, Uta. 2007. *Making Up the Mind: How the Brain Creates Our Mental World*. Oxford: Blackwell Publishing.

Gay, Peter. 1995. *The Freud Reader*. New York: Norton.

Gilbert, C. 2012. "Intermediate-level visual processing and visual primitives." In *Principles of Neural Science*, 5th ed., edited by Kandel et al. 2012:602-620.

Gombrich, Ernst H. 1960. *Art and Illusion: A Study in the Psychology of Pictorial Representation*. London: Phaidon.

Gombrich, Ernst H. 1982. *The Image and the Eye: Further Studies in the Psychology of Pictorial Representation*. London: Phaidon.

Gombrich, Ernst H. 1984. "Reminiscences on Collaboration with Ernst Kris (1900-1957)." In *Tributes: Interpreters of Our Cultural Tradition*. Ithaca, NY: Cornell University Press.

Gombrich, Ernst H. and Kris, Ernst. 1940. *Caricature*. London: King Penguin Books.

Gombrich, Ernst H. and Kris, Ernst. 1999. "The Principles of Caricature." *British Journal of Medical Psychology* 17L319-342. In: *Psychoanalytic Explorations in Art*.

Gregory, Richard L. 2009. *Seeing Through Illusions*. New York: Oxford University Press.

Hubel, David and Wiesel, Torsten. 2005. *Brain and a Visual Perception: The story of a 25 year collaboration*. New York: Oxford University Press.

Kandel, Eric R. 2012. *The Age of Insight: The Quest to Understand the Unconscious in Art, Mind, and Brain From Vienna 1900 to the Present*. New York: Random House.

Kallir, J. and Schoenberg, A. 1984. *Arnold Schoenberg's Vienna*. New York: Galerie St. Etienne/Rizzoli.

Kemp, W. 2000. Introduction to Riegl, Alois. 1902. *The Group Portraiture of Holland*. Translated by EM Kain, D Britt. Los Angeles, CA: Getty Center for the History of Art and Humanities.

Kobatake, E., Tanaka, K. 1994. "Neuronal selectivities to complex object features in the ventral visual pathway of the macaque cerebral cortex." *J. Neurophysiol.* 71 (3):856-2280.

Kris, Ernst. 1936. "The Psychology of Caricature." *International Journal of Psycho-Analysis* 17:285-303.

Kris, Ernst. 1952. "Aesthetic Ambiguity." In: *Psychoanalytic Explorations in Art*. New York: International University Press.

Kris, Ernst. 1952. "A Psychotic Sculptor of the Eighteenth Century." In: *Psychoanalytic Explorations in Art*. New York: International University Press.

Kris, Ernst. 1952. *Psychoanalytic Explorations in Art*. New York: International University Press.

Miyashita, Yasushi, et al. 1998. "Consolidation of Visual Associative Long-Term Memory in the Temporal Cortex of Primates." *Neurobiology of Learning and Memory*, 70:197-211.

Purves, Dale and R. Beau Lotto. 2010. *Why We See What We Do Redux: A Wholly Empirical Theory of Vision*. Sunderland, MA: Sinauer Associates.

Riegl, Alois. 2000. *The Group Portraiture of Holland*. Translated by E. M. Kain, D. Britt. Originally published in 1902.

Rose, Louis. 2007. "Daumier in Vienna: Ernst Kris, E.H. Gombrich, and the Politics of Caricature." *Visual Resources* 23(1-2):39-64.

Rose, Louis. In Press. *Psychology, Art, and Antifacism: Ernst Kris, E.H. Gombrich, and the Caricature Project*.

Schapiro, Meyer. 1994. *Theory and Philosophy of Art: Style, Artist, and Society*. New York: George Braziller.

Schapiro, Meyer. 2000. "The New Viennese School." In: *The Vienna School Reader*. Edited by C Wood. New York: Zone Books. Originally published in 1936.

Scharf, Alfred. 1935. *Fillipino Lippi*. Vienna 1935 p. 92.

Thompson, P. 1980. "Margaret Thatcher: a new illusion." *Perception*, 9: 483-484.

Tsao, Doris Y. et al. 2008. "Comparing face patch systems in macaques and humans." *PNAS*. 49:19514-9.

West, Shearer. 2004. *Portraiture*. Oxford History of Art. Oxford University Press.

Zeki, Semir. 1993. *A Vision of the Brain*. Blackwell Scientific Publications: Oxford

Zucker, Paul. 1963. *Stages in Painting. A Comparative Study*. Dover Publications, Inc: New York.

Acknowledgments

I thank Alessandra Comini for her comments on an earlier draft of this essay. I also am indebted to Blair Potter, whose superb editing guided my writing of *The Age of Insight* and who brought her wonderful insights to bear on this essay. I owe a debt to my colleague Chris Willcox, who helped me put the art program for this essay together, and to Pauline Henick for typing this manuscript.

Ashley and I have been collecting art for 15 years. While we've collected pieces from a lot of different artists, Vik Muniz has always been one of our favorites. We both fell in love with Vik's work and his use of ordinary objects in creating whimsical and iconic images. We've collected pieces from many of his series that use items such as thread, wire, soil, chocolate, magazine clippings, and, of course, diamonds. There are a number of portraits in his diamond series, but we particularly liked the apt combination of diamonds and Marilyn Monroe. We enjoy art that is fun, and this piece expresses what can be the playful nature and livability of contemporary art.

Jim Diamond
Collector

Appropriate is the word that comes to mind in describing my reaction to the photograph of Marilyn Monroe by Vik Muniz. The word serves several purposes. Appropriating diamonds to create the portrait forms an alluring juxtaposition. Diamonds are cold, Marilyn is hot. In another way, diamonds and Marilyn are appropriate together. Diamonds are a symbol of glamour, desirability, and beauty—qualities that could also describe Marilyn. Then there is the song, "Diamonds are a Girl's Best Friend" that Marilyn sings in the movie *Gentlemen Prefer Blondes*. First and foremost, the image is appropriated from Andy Warhol. I'm not sure how I feel about artists who use different materials with someone else's artwork. Should appropriation be considered an original work of art? Does familiarity breed contempt? In questioning all these facets (pun intended), the work becomes more engaging.

GG Kopilak
Artist and TV host

Franz Pourbus the Younger (1569-1622)
Duke of Mantua, ca. 1600
Oil on canvas
32 x 25 inches
Private collection
Photo: Margaret Fox

Well, the first thing I thought of when I saw this painting was Colin Firth, not in his Mr. Darcy incarnation, but as the cuckolded husband in *Shakespeare in Love*. Must've been the ruffled collar, plus I was reading about him earlier in the day. Funny how the mind works. But then I was drawn to the curtain, and I wondered, who's this gent waiting on? Why me, of course. I'm a lady-in-waiting at the court. Or maybe I'm a queen. (I certainly think of myself as a queen.) Will I say 'yes' or will I say 'no' in this secret rendezvous? I'm not certain. The only thing that is certain is the conversation will continue among the artist, the subject, and the viewer.

Georgette Gouveia
Editor, *WAG Magazine*

That millstone collar sure shows off the sitter's face and makes him look handsome and rich, which was of course the intent. Since I immediately wondered how the collar was made, washed, and starched, I looked it up and now know that it took about ten yards of linen to gather in the ruff, and a "goffering iron" to create the figure-eight pleats, and that Lutheran ministers in Scandinavia still wear them to this day.

As impressive as the collar is, so are the Duke of Mantua's eyes. He looks approachable rather than haughty, ready to have a conversation. The painter used all the trappings—from the draped red curtain, to the collar, to the armor he wears—to portray the Duke as the important man he must have been.

Peter G. Rose
Author/Food Historian

Little Punch or How I Bought Folk Art from Howard Finster

In 1984 I was in Somerville, Georgia, and I bought *Little Punch* from Howard Finster. We were four people from the Katonah Museum of Art, and we were researching Outsider Art for an exhibition titled *Beyond Tradition: Contemporary American Folk Art.* We visited artists and galleries and kept our appointment with Finster at his Folk Art Church, which was jam-packed with his paintings, sculptures, assemblages, and a profusion of found objects. Hardly an empty space to be seen.

Amid this claustrophobic accumulation, I spotted *Little Punch,* placed on its side on the floor, and I asked about it. The artist stood it upright and explained that it was just completed. It was copied from a photograph of his wife's little brother who, sadly, was killed at the age of five by an automobile. The painting brought to mind the simple figures and distinctive colors of a work that has always intrigued me: *Music,* by Pierre Matisse.

When I indicated that I would be interested in buying *Little Punch*, Finster told me he had painted it for his wife, Pauline, and would be happy to paint another for me. I countered that I was not in the habit of buying art without seeing it. "Well," he said, "I'll ask Pauline if I can sell this one." A quick phone call and Pauline said she was thrilled that someone would like to have a painting of her little brother. So the deal was made.

Not so fast. The painting was not quite finished. Finster personalized each of his works with a date, a sequential number, and a religious reference. So I watched as he painted the information in a bottom corner of the picture. A prolific artist, Finster recorded it among his works as number 3,572. In a frame with a simple folksy design, the painting was wrapped in heavy brown paper and ready to go. I carried it to the airport and home, and have enjoyed *Little Punch* ever since.

Private Collector

WELL WE KNOW
WHERE WE'RE GOIN'
BUT WE DON'T KNOW
WHERE WE'VE BEEN
AND WE KNOW WHAT
WE'RE KNOWIN'
BUT WE CAN'T SAY
WHAT WE'VE SEEN

Lyrics from *The Road to Nowhere* by the Talking Heads

For me the soundtrack to any Howard Finster painting is the Talking Heads. Although he designed covers for many bands, the Talking Heads *Little Creatures* album was the first Finster image I ever saw. Without knowing who had created it, I began to see his artwork everywhere—it jumped out at you with that immediately recognizable style. I was studying art history in the 80's and Finster's work was jarring next to the "fine art" of the older time periods. Was this folk art from long ago or something contemporary with the reemergence of figurative art? If the term Outsider Art even existed at the time, it wasn't something I was learning about in school, but here it was on the album cover of one of the coolest New Wave bands around. It must be great art, after all David Byrne had gone to RISD and the Talking Heads played CBGBs.

So, who is Little Punch? Is this a portrait of a real person or one of Finster's figures from religious history? In that white shift is Punch a boy, a girl, or something in between—an angel perhaps? At first look I saw the blue as sky and the green as grass, like any child coloring a picture would draw. But as I looked closer, the divide between sky and land comes right at the waist; perhaps that's not green grass, but blue-green water? The legs that looked awkward for standing are graceful for floating; the hands might be paddling or churning. But that face, it is not happy and not sad—what emotion is that? Perhaps trepidation? And there it is, a figure plunging into the water, a baptism, some form of purification, but caught in that moment of time between past and future, lost and saved, in and out, good and evil. What will become of Little Punch and, for that matter, who is Big Punch?

Michael Clark
Hackley Lower School Librarian

Howard Finster (1916-2001)
Little Punch, 1984
Paint on wood
56 x 24 inches
Private collection
Photo: Margaret Fox

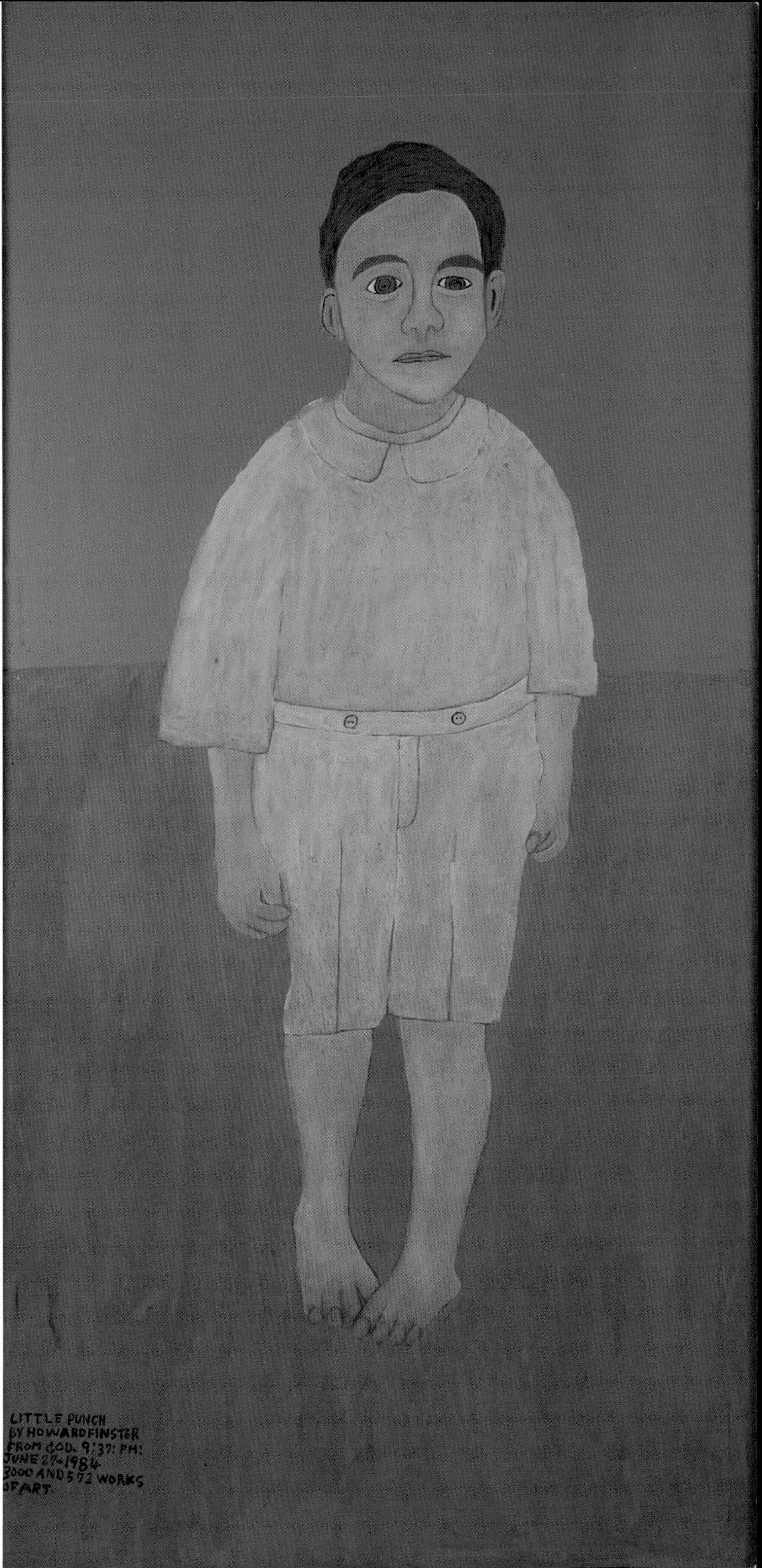
LITTLE PUNCH
BY HOWARD FINSTER
FROM GOD. 9:37: PM:
JUNE 27-1984
3000 AND 572 WORKS
OF ART.

Gustave Courbet (1819-1877)
Portrait of Jo, 1865
Oil on paper, mounted on mahogany board
10.625 x 8.5 inches
Private collection
Photo: Margaret Fox

This small, intimate, freely-painted canvas has deep personal appeal. Jo—as mistress to James Abbott McNeill Whistler and muse to Gustave Courbet—was a robust, fun-loving, young Irish woman. This work portrays Jo as she most probably was naturally. Courbet's intense obsession with her hair (later developed in the larger 1866 painting of Jo at the Metropolitan) is clearly seen in the application of paint. She is enveloped by her rich, sensual hair, natural and tousled, so prominent it is almost the subject.

In this intimate portrait—a vignette—Jo is crowded into the small space and tenderly rendered. The paleness of garment and background is soft and fresh, and of the sea. The artist painted this in Trouville on the Normandy coast after leaving the dark forest of the Franche-Comté. Courbet has captured Jo in an unguarded moment with such tenderness that one has to wonder if he was just a little in love with her himself.

Private Collector

I detect the faintest halo around Jo's red head—although this favorite model, muse, and mistress of both Gustave Courbet and James Abbott McNeill Whistler would be the first to admit—she was no angel. Whistler's mother (yes, that one) didn't approve. All the more reason to admire this working-class lass whose full name was Joanna Hiffernan.

Besides the model for this Realist portrait—with broad brushstrokes, her facing away—she's also Courbet's *La Belle Irlandaise* at the Met, where she's stroking her famously voluptuous coppery waves. She also sat for Courbet's most controversial nude, *L'Origine du Monde*. There's Jo again in Whistler's iconic *Symphony in White, No 1: The White Girl*. While Ireland was still reeling from the Great Famine, this plucky Irish girl was making her way around the ateliers of Paris and London. As her hair color attests: a girl on fire.

Joyce Corrigan
Author and contributing editor
to *Marie Claire*

Igbo (Ibo) tribe, Nigeria
Maiden Spirit Mask, 1903
Painted wood
18 inches high
Arctic Artistry Gallery
Photo: Margaret Fox

Scary! I don't like the sharp teeth and empty eyes. I would freak out if the mask was in my house.

It's very detailed—everything is outlined. It must be heavy to wear. I wonder why the mask is for a girl because the face looks like a grown man's.

Malina Kern
Age 12

My first reaction to this mask, other than 'wow, nice Mohawk,' is that it must have been very heavy to wear—especially if it was meant for a young, adolescent girl. The expression strikes me as emotionally ambivalent. It could be angry (look at those bared teeth) or is that a slight smile? Maybe those are tears streaming down from the eyes? Now that I think about it, the range of expression present in that face is pretty appropriate for an adolescent girl. You're not certain which way it will go and it could change at any moment.

Humor aside, I love the mouth. Apart from the elaborate headdress, which is mighty impressive, the mouth is fierce. It's so much more detailed—each tooth carefully cut out—compared with the very basic carving of the other facial features. I wonder if it was intentional or if the maker was just good at teeth.

Peter Linz
Puppeteer

21

Kehinde Wiley (b. 1977)
Morthyn Brito, 2011
Oil on linen
60 x 50 inches
The Albert Laboz Family Collection
© Kehinde Wiley and Sean Kelly,
New York, New York

Colors. I am infused and immersed in color. No matter what you might think of me, color surrounds me and excites me. No matter what you might think of my colors, they are strong and beautiful and radiant. These flowers surround me, their branches extending, flowing, evolving, telling a story, my story. I wear these colors proudly. Can't you see? Who is that you see on my jacket? What part does he play in my magnificent story of color? The yellows, greens, blues, browns, whites, oranges, black, all shades that bring life to me. All a part of me. Can't you see? We try to place colors into boxes. We separate the colors by shade, tone, and vibrancy, but together we make a beautiful story. Can't you see?

Dierdra Gray Clark
Minister

This portrait is vibrant and full of contradictions. The subject has a man's confrontational stare with a boy's frightened eyes. He looks like a wounded prince in a soft quilted jacket. The skin is so real and sensual that it glows. The light on his ear is stunning, but the artist doesn't mask the knot and scar on his forehead. The shadow over his eye hides something. It's intriguing.

The clothes beg for attention and contradict the flat wallpaper. The background is beautiful, but seems contrived compared to the soft detailed jacket. The vines are literally creeping over him, pulling him into the background.

I think this painting is about identity; about coming out. I think there is a struggle between his background and the way he wants to be seen. The truth is in his eyes. He's challenged and afraid despite his bold beauty. It looks like the word "love" is peeking through his jacket—not ready for public viewing.

Allison Daugherty
Actress

Effacement

How does loss contribute to more? Your brain works feverishly to fill in the missing details, details eroded from countless journeys that connect us to a time so far removed from today. Chips, scratches, and breaks force us to finish Amenhotep in our minds, with a resolution as strong as if it were chiseled yesterday. We dream of circumstances that led to the Cartesian break of head from body. But this six-inch epic of basalt solemnity will not reveal its secrets. His expression captures the fortitude and solidity of a ruler who presided over one of the peaks of Egyptian dynasties. Or rather, it is his distinct absence of expression that makes him so timeless. A man, a king, and perhaps a deity to his contemporaries. In the end we are left with more because of less.

Eric Finzi, MD
Artist and plastic surgeon

The small bust of Amenhotep III sits on the edge of my desk. I see it almost every day. I originally purchased it at auction in 1994 after my 45-year career as a professor of Egyptian history at Yale and as an Egyptologist leading archeological excavations. The dark stone carving of the young, handsome king is arresting, but often I hardly notice him, like an old shoe that no longer fits. It is a reminder of what used to be, the excitement of scholarship, the discovery of ancient treasures in Egypt, the translation of hieroglyphics—all memories of the past.

Amenhotep III began his reign as a boy of twelve and ruled for over 38 years during a period of great prosperity, peace, and cultural glory. When I use my imagination and fill in the erosion of time, I see a sweet sensual face with individual personality despite the usual stylization of Egyptian art. This is a rare portrait of the king as a young man before his accomplishments as the pharaoh that beautified Egypt and used diplomacy to enhance national power. He built many monuments and added splendor to Luxor and Karnak. Although it is believed that he had more than 300 wives, his Great Royal Wife and favorite was Tiye. Imagine having 300 competitors.

William Kelly Simpson
Collector

A Japanese man
Posing as Mona Lisa?
    Let's ask a white guy!

I could've done this.
Take a pic and photoshop...
    But...
        He did it.
            First...

You call this real art?
    Defacing a Masterpiece...
    ...hmmm...intriguing smile...

He's kind of pretty.
Wait, a guy can't think that stuff!
Now I'm all confused...

Scott Fauver
Bedford, NY resident

The idea of appropriated art is about a century old, but for many artists and laypersons, the jury is still out, if not hopelessly deadlocked. Here, the puckish Japanese photographer Yasumasa Morimura has fashioned his own face, open expression, and hands ("a selfie," in downtown lingo) as Leonardo's emotionally indeterminate Mona Lisa. The dimensions of the works are almost precisely the same, purposely making comparisons literal. But to what purpose? Skeptics might grouse that the painter supposedly labored for four years off and on to produce the original; Morimura, uh, did not. Does that matter?

In *Elliott Erwitt's Handbook* (2003), I wrote, "Although we speak of the `Mona Lisa smile,' painters note the `Gioconda pose' [of the hands] as the true focal point." Why, then, the subtle differences between those original hands and Morimura's, notably the left one? Or of the Asian black hair replacing Leonardo's subject's north Italian wavy locks? Is it mere coincidence that the background in both pieces has been described as reflecting Far Eastern (specifically Chinese, not Japanese) influence? Leonardo used oil on wood; his appropriator, photographic image on canvas. So?

For advocates of appropriation, such questions are the burning points. A "new" work uses the existing object to make or provoke fresh observations. Let the jury of Morimura's peers decide.

Charles Flowers
Author

Over the past fifty years I have been commissioned to execute numerous portraits. The second challenge after creating a desired likeness is just what to do with the eyes, especially if the subject is a frontal portrait. What should the eyes convey to the viewer? Is Edouard Vuillard's gaze in his *Self-Portrait with Cane and Straw Hat* asking one to return his stare? Is he coming out to greet or invite one in?

There is so much depth in those simple shapes that stand in for eyes. They are the same color and value as the irregular shapes in the painting's background. In addition, Vuillard's placement of textured panels of color and his hat sitting squarely on his head both play an emotional role. Even when we pry ourselves away from his face, and make our way around the rest of the canvas, his yellow canc points us back to his face, and once again to those eyes.

Jerry Pinkney
Narrative Artist

This intimate portrait of the young Edouard Vuillard captures him at the instant he enters a doorway, a possible metaphor for his arrival into the Parisian avant-garde and his burgeoning association with a circle of contemporary French intellectuals. His illustrious career has just begun. A point underscored by the fact that his left shoulder and hat brim remain partially hidden behind the doorjamb. He has not fully emerged; there will be more to come.

This painting is a snapshot sketch revealing his passion for photography as a visual tool, informing him of compositional possibilities and the cognitive power of suggestion. The warmth of his color selection, painted with inspired confidence in a loose and rapid manner, beckons the viewer with the promise of a personal introduction, only to find that Vuillard reveals little about himself with one potential exception. The golden radiance backlighting his figure functions as an aura implying, at the very least, his personal belief in a brilliant future.

Creighton Michael
Artist

As I observe this photograph, I imagine that Frida Kahlo will look over at me at any moment. It seems odd to me that she would be gazing away from the camera. She was the kind of person who would look you straight in the eye and tell you exactly what was on her mind. What would be on her mind today? I think she might reflect on the world and feel dismayed at the inequities, she would celebrate the increased opportunities young women have, and she would be appalled that families are torn apart by massive numbers of deportations. Maybe she knew some of what was to come, and this is precisely why she doesn't look me in the eye.

Carola Otero Bracco
Executive Director, Neighbors
Link Northern Westchester

The first time I saw Carl Van Vechten's photograph of Frida Kahlo, I was struck by her statuesque bearing and her air of confidence despite her averted gaze. Frida's bold jewelry and decorative clothing suggest a strong sense of style, but her severe hairstyle adds a note of restraint.

Frida's serious expression makes her seem to be contemplating something in the distance, but on closer inspection, she appears somber, almost melancholy. There is definitely an aura of mystery to this fascinating portrait, enticing one to find out much more about this interesting lady!

Lee Roberts
Bedford Town Supervisor

How well can this Gloria evoke feelings that she had years ago when wearing a printed dress and painted skin, much like Oliver Herring's *Gloria*? How young in heart, soul, and mind was I when my kinky hair, in a natural state, was picked with an Afro comb to as big a size as this young woman could manage? In those free-style days of banishing bras, I now wish that I had been solely committed to the civil rights of Afro-American families in America, our brothers and sisters around the world, living things, and planet earth. Today I realize that the past was a stepping stone on a lifelong path that has led to a spiritual state of loving all that the Creator has entrusted to our care. I wonder if these sacred things are on the mind of Mr. Herring's *Gloria*, and those pondering her?

Gloria Jean Pinkney
Author

I love *Gloria*, always have. I never met the woman from whom she is modeled, but Oliver Herring has.

This body of work is my favorite example of Oliver's compassionate and deeply felt reaction to the people with whom he works in both his static and performance art. It is through the lengthy process of photographing, molding the work, and then coating it with pieces of photographs of the subject that Oliver gets "under the skin" and so deeply reveals Gloria.

He combines the disciplines of photography and sculpture in a way that expands the power of both.

I bought *Gloria* out of Oliver's show at the Max Protetch Gallery in 2004 or '05.

Max Protetch
Collector

27

Cecil Beaton (1904-1980)
Portrait of Lucie B. Rosen, ca. 1932
Pencil, watercolor, and gouache on paper
16.5 x 11.5 inches
Caramoor Rosen House Collection

"**W**ell, hello, I am quite beautiful, do you appreciate this?"

Lucie Rosen's enigmatic look illustrates her unique charm and power over people. Here she looks ravishingly delicate in a yellow gown that accentuates her swan neck, pencil-thin arms, and erect posture. Her figure declares "I am the mistress of the house and the evening."

Lucie's choice of gown echoes the sparkling crystals of the candelabra with the ones sewn into her dress. Will this soirée be a grand party or an intimate dinner for two? She is certainly not greeting anyone with a smile or gesture of welcome. She is the queen of the manor, and the night will be hers to orchestrate.

Judy Evnin
Chairman Emerita, Caramoor

Cecil Beaton is lauded as "the greatest fashion and portrait photographer of his time." For 60 years, he captured "everyone who was anyone" in the worlds of high society, theatre, and glamour. Of course, the beautiful and wealthy Lucie Rosen would be one of his subjects! However, the delightful discovery in this depiction of grace and elegance is the *conspiratorial cheekiness* of it. And isn't that what good portraiture is all about: a surprising insight into one's public face? Lucie's classical stance and gold bejeweled gown bespeak *hauteur*, but the statues beside the hearth convey something else entirely. Those naughty 'mooning' nudes (so PBS Mystery!, Edward Gorey-ish) are not-so-subtly poking fun at all this pretense and pomposity, and Lucie is in on the joke. Beaton inserts his image into her *mirror* (symbol of her conscience?), his eyes and nose cannily reminiscent of "Kilroy was here." Perhaps Cocteau was right. Cecil, he said, was "Malice in Wonderland."

Rosita Benson
KMA Docent

Indian, Master of the School of Mankot
Portrait of Raja Mahipat Dev
ca. 1690-1710
7.5 x 11 inches
Opaque watercolor on paper
David Swope
Photo: Margaret Fox

It's hard to tell if the night is about to begin or about to end for the Maharaja. He looks deep in thought—in anticipation of what is to come or reflective about what has already happened? The wine is clearly special, a wine of kings, no doubt. There have been many of those throughout the world's history of wine and kings. With the golden walls, the bright green of his wardrobe, and those brilliant drops at his fingertips, I think this might be a very grand white wine of great body and flavor—complex, elegant, deep, and thoughtful—much like the Maharaja himself. Could this be a chalice of the Corton-Charlemagne of India? I would like to think so. And I would also like to think the evening is only about to begin. Perhaps a feast of amazing food, wine, and women? An evening fit for a king. It's good to be the king.

Glenn Vogt
Partner and Wine Director
Crabtree's Kittle House
RiverMarket Bar & Kitchen

I found this painting in Bombay in 1968 when I was a volunteer in India serving in the Peace Corps. I was drawn to it by its honesty and simplicity, which suggested to me the distilled essence expressed by mold-breaking artists of the 20th century.

The painting portrays Raja Mahipat Dev of Mankot seated in prayer. The composition is strong, bold, and stunningly simple. It is unadorned by the trappings of royalty. The colors are less pretty than they are expressive (the ochre-colored background is typical of the Mankot school). The mountainous hill station from which this painting originates is small, remote, and not far from Dharamsala where the Dalai Lama presently lives in the low foothills of the Himalayas.

The portrait hangs in my front hall where I pass it daily. I loved it 45 years ago, and I still do.

David Swope
Collector

29

Benjamin West (1738-1820)
Portrait of the Artist's Sons, Raphael West and Benjamin West Jr., Playing with Dogs, 1775
Oil on canvas
41 x 31.5 inches
Private collection

Being a parent is awe-inspiring, profound, and at times truly bittersweet. Given my new status as an "empty nester," I'm deeply aware of this and my heart aches with how fast our girls have grown up. Benjamin West portrays the aching joy of parenthood in every note of this work. The purity of childhood is highlighted by the boys' loving embrace that spirals to the heavens. The clear and bright light bathing them further suggests this divine state and the younger son is cherubic with his heavenly glance and a wrap suggestive of an angel wing. The older son is a step ahead on the path of life: in adult dress, looking downward, protective of his angelic brother. Even the full-bloom rose suggests the passing purity of childhood. West captures the fleeting state of childhood grace and the attendant blessings that every parent savors over a lifetime.

Leslie Needham
Landscape Designer

When I first glanced at this portrait by Benjamin West on my smartphone, I was co-piloting my family's northern excursion to Bar Harbor, Maine. As it was a thumbprint of its actual size, I misjudged the image to be one of a mother, child, and puppy, not a portrait of the artist's two sons. In that moment, however, I felt an internal surge of joy tinged with just enough melancholy to bring tears to my eyes.

"Mom, what's the matter?" my ever-sensitive daughter called out from the backseat. I took a moment to show my children the image on my iPhone. I reminded them of a time when they too traipsed around in the buff and were easily delighted with life's simplicity.

Upon returning from our travels, I pulled the image up on my desktop where in its larger presentation I could see that the exchange was obviously between siblings. Though my reaction was decidedly less intimate, it was no less refreshing. I laughed out loud at the moment of utter joy captured on canvas, knowing that even in 1775, Mr. West's sons following years would bring dips of strife that would leave the artist clinging to this image, just as I reflect upon happy moments, now caught on camera, between my children.

My separate reactions inform me that art is not only in the eye of the beholder, but that true art never stands still. Perhaps by definition art is constantly revealing, speaking to us all with the more time we give to it.

I look forward to seeing the original painting at the Katonah Museum of Art in October and all the other portraits they've collected. In fact, I can't wait!

Sarah Hodgson
Huffington Post Blogger and local Dog Trainer

Gordon Parks (1912-2006)
Little Richard, Harlem, New York, 1967
Archival pigment print
14 x 11 inches
Courtesy The Gordon Parks Foundation
© The Gordon Parks Foundation

Questions For Richard

Even young children know so much. Yet, your gaze leaves me wondering what your dark eyes saw. Was a loving family able to give you shelter, clothing, and food enough? Life may be hard, but did you feel secure? Courage to face the world is tended at the hearth of love. Did you feel that love and were you heard? Were your words treasured above the rabble of the day? With compassion in your eyes, did your little feet run to help a friend or brother? The gift of empathy builds self-worth. Did you step forth in confidence to learn all that you could? Oh, I hope so, for therein lies the power to become.

Your times and circumstances may have been difficult, but I do hope you fared well, that you are happy and strong in spite of the inevitable bruises of a full life.

Gwen Kopeinig
Teacher
Lewisboro Elementary School

Born into poverty and segregation in Kansas in 1912, Gordon Parks was drawn to photography as a young man when he saw images of migrant workers published in a magazine left behind on a train where he worked as a waiter. He bought a camera at a pawnshop and taught himself how to use it. Despite his lack of professional training, Parks quickly developed the style that would make him one of the most celebrated photographers of his era. In the 1950s, as the first African-American staff photographer at *Life* magazine, his reputation grew exponentially as he covered stories no one else could, on a wide range of subjects, from racism and poverty to fashion.

Parks is remembered for the great narrative photo essays he produced for *Life* between 1948 and 1970. *The Fontenelles* may be one of his finest picture stories, revealing the intimate lives of a poor family in Harlem in 1967. Made to illustrate larger patterns of poverty to a mainstream audience, Parks's photographs shocked America's conscience when they appeared in the pages of the country's best-selling magazine. Gordon Parks was a humanitarian who was trusted by his subjects and who used his camera to help tell very personal stories.

Peter W. Kunhardt, Jr.
Executive Director
The Gordon Parks Foundation

Mende, Sierra Leone
Dance Mask, Early 20th century
Carved wood
14.5 inches high
Bruce Frank Primitive Art
Photo: Oren Eckhaus

When I look at this mask I see strength in women. It is a symbol for women to be strong for their families. It speaks to all women no matter what their age, religion, or race. Since women are considered to be Mother Earth, like the lioness she must give birth, provide, and protect. Her eyes show wisdom. Her smile shows kindness. Her forehead shows cunningness. Her hair is neatly woven to display her vanity and feminine beauty. Masks can be used for masquerade or to ward off evil or just as plain cover-up. I think this mask could have all three uses.

Joseph DiMauro
Mt. Kisco Seafood

A mask can be a roadmap to the experience of a people. It can lead us on journeys that tell of joyful ceremonies and meaningful rituals. Its materials, colors, patterns, and textures reveal a society's geography and aesthetic. And its expression can clearly signal the emotional significance of an event.

The Mende Dance Mask is like the Mona Lisa of dance masks. It is a beautifully crafted mask, but it is mysterious to me, suggesting more questions than answers. Both the serene expression and elegant symmetry offer no information about the occasion or the purpose of the dance. Is the dance celebratory or somber? Is the mask used for an annual event or a rite of passage? An important religious observance? The story is concealed behind the mask's peaceful countenance.

And what would this dance look like? What sort of music would be played? I am curious about the rest of the costume that would be worn for this dance. What are the colors and patterns? I wonder if the dancer would be solitary or perform in a group, and I try to imagine how the dancer would move across space.

I am left wanting to learn much more.

Wendy Isler Alvarez
Artist and retired Art Teacher
Katonah-Lewisboro Schools

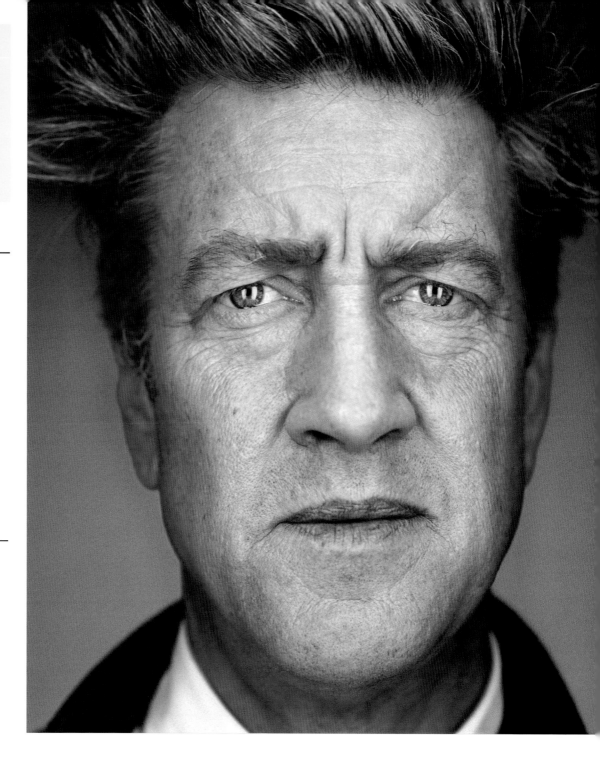

Why am I here?
What am I doing?
Who did my hair?
I feel as though my life is a dream,
or a nightmare. Is there really
much difference? And who cares?

Eve Marx
Author, *Beddington Place: Watch
Your Back, Cover Your Tracks*
Columnist & Feature Writer, *The
Bedford Record Review* and
Bedford Magazine contributor

Looks like a boss, doesn't he? A
boss who is about to fire someone.
He needs some Botox, but he has
nice eyes and a good shave.

His hairstyle appears much younger
than his face. He's probably been
around young people a lot and
wants to fit in. I don't think I'd like to
be married to him.

**Marjie Kern
President, Katonah Museum
Artists' Association**

Byron Kim (b. 1961)
Emmett at Twelve Months, 1994
Egg tempera on panel
Suite of 25 paintings
3 x 2.5 x .75 inches each
17 x 14.5 x .75 inches
Courtesy of the artist and James Cohan
Gallery, New York / Shanghai

I don't see the twelve-month-old in these cubes of color. I can see that the colors are warm, but I find the painting as a portrait cold and unsatisfying, without love or human relationship. It's not a painting I'm able to relate to because I'm more of a traditionalist in art.

Diana Tyler
Proprietor
Kelloggs and Lawrence Hardware

If I were to come upon this painting outside of the context of this exhibition, with no knowledge of the artist's body of work, and with no way of learning its title, I would enjoy it aesthetically. Indeed, the work is notable for the subtlety of the palette, the delicate surface of each small canvas, and the harmonious proportions of the parts and their sum.

However, knowing the context, the artist, and the title, I am in the enjoyable position of evaluating the work as the portrait of a child.

I assume that the hue of each canvas represents a color that the artist observed when carefully scrutinizing his son Emmett. Therefore, when I look at this portrait, I see the variations in his skin tone and the colors of his eyes, hair, teeth, and lips. This process makes me smile, for I can well remember the pleasures of staring at my two sons, when they were small and peacefully asleep.

Marcy B. Freedman
Artist and Art Historian

Tchambuli Culture (New Guinea, on the Aibom Lake)
Portrait Head, Early 20th century
Wood, pigment, and shell
11.125 x 6.375 x 6.875 inches
1933 Expedition, Dr. Margaret Mead
American Museum of Natural History
(80.0/7377)

I am an art conservator. When I look at any piece of art, I am always aware of the passage of time and how a work has changed since its creation. The Tchambuli head has faint marks of white paint, but the impact of the face paint is much weaker than on other similar sculptures that have more of their paint intact. I wonder why this mask was chosen over the others. Does this one look more "human" and therefore more appealing to us than others, where the swirling, high-contrasting lines create a design of their own and make it difficult to "see" the face beneath?

**Barbara Appelbaum
Art Conservator**

I look at the wood portrait that Margaret Mead brought back from New Guinea in 1933, the year I was in utero, and I see mostly staring, maybe slightly exotropic eyes without much revealing of the subject other than perhaps seriousness of purpose. And suggestive of some evidence, according to Mead, of the role of women in the Tchambuli tribes she studied.

The portrait shows the shaved head, assumed by women in that culture, the mouth and cheeks show a facial expression not so much as dominance to me (another concept of Mead's for women), but of simply paying attention and yes, certainly without mirth or frivolity. There appears to be some adornment, with paint on the forehead and cheeks, but less perhaps than we know of the men in the tribes in New Guinea, not however confirming that men did more self-adornment than women.

This woodcut is a good depiction of a Tchambuli woman. To attribute too much to it about the influence of culture on gender roles, as Margaret Mead did, might be a bit too far-reaching. One would almost have to have lived half one's life as a man and the other half as a woman to comment on that.

**Renee Richards, MD
Ophthalmologist**

Louis-Léopold Boilly (1761-1845)
Grimacing Man (Self-Portrait), ca. 1822-23
Black chalk with touches of white and
red chalk on light brown (formerly blue)
wove paper
9.75 x 7.75 inches
Private collection

Ha! What is so striking to me about this portrait is the purely childish spirit of this guy, winking goofily at us across the centuries. The formal portraiture of the Old Masters seems almost like a conspiracy to hide the fact that even way back then, we enjoyed acting like a jackass from time to time.

Peter de Sève
Illustrator

This 1822 portrait of a *Grimacing Man* by Louis-Léopold Boilly bears the distinct appearance of a snapshot. It seems to capture the essence of a particular moment, a split second, a fleeting expression frozen in time. This is rare in works created before the advent of photography, about 1840. Early portraits were almost always the products of many days, or even weeks, of the subject sitting motionless before the artist. Finished portraits (whether painted or sketched) rarely captured the sense of reality —the immediacy of a given moment that photography would later provide. As such, this is a unique work—a precursor of a new world just beyond the horizon.

Neil Waldman
Illustrator

Julian Opie (b. 1958)
This is Monique, 2004
Continuous computer animation,
computer film, PC, and 19-inch LCD
screen, Edition 4 of 4
Private collection
Courtesy of Barbara Krakow
Gallery, Boston

I think I have a new friend. I love talking to Monique. I can let off steam, tell her a joke or a story and she is THERE for me. My bichon, Edelweiss, is weary of me.... I would like to have Monique in my kitchen on a cabinet so as I do my chores I can bounce things off of her. She reminds me of my Patrician friends. Very *Preppy Handbook*. She is well groomed—fresh-faced but great attention is paid to her hair—healthy as a horse's mane. Sunglasses atop her head, rather than a black hairband, and pearl earrings instead of a pearl necklace (although she has the perfect neckline for it) tells me that she simply had to rush over to hear what I had to say. Her expressions are numerous yet she never wrinkles her brow—smart girl!

Karen Benvin Ransom
KMA Volunteer

Gazing at Monique I immediately see my mother circa 1966. She's just walked into our bathroom and found my seven-year-old self standing in front of the mirror attempting to draw in the eyebrows I'd just so carelessly shaved off. I couldn't imagine why our creator had added them; they seemed such an unnecessary facial feature. Once off, however, I understand all too well that our eyebrows are the windows to our soul. Two rather simple, non-descript lines; yet they seemingly hold the rest of our facial features together and bring a wide range of emotion to an otherwise blank canvas. Rather than scolding me (trust me, being eyebrow-less was punishment enough), my mother slowly raises and then lowers her eyebrows and her message is delivered loud and clear—ouch! That's the day I learned that a simple line could mean nothing or everything. It's all about one's interpretation.

Martha Handler
Writer

This appears to me to be a seaside portrait. The yellow lines represent the sun and the patterned fabric at the bottom of the portrait perhaps a picnic cloth? I see the cigarette and beret as a counterpoint to what I see as the "brain" inside the head. The image seems busy, almost chaotic. I recognize the symbol of a fish, just next to his right eye. Do you think the great master could actually be in the midst of self-reflection? While appearing cool and collected on the outside (relaxing with a cigarette), I see significant turmoil in his head. To me, the beard and hair symbolize his virility and need to appear youthful. Perhaps this is a Picasso in transition, having been left by another mistress and beginning a new and different period in his creative life.

Sharon Kreiger, MD
Internal Medicine

Pablo Picasso's bearded man smoking a cigarette casts an agitated glance at something off in the distance, or perhaps he is looking at me. Filled with an energy conveyed through vibrant, contrasting colors and quick, spontaneous lines, the artist's drawing offers a glimpse of both the inner and outer man. Emotion and the physicality of subject are combined in this work, provoking a strong visceral response. We are reminded of the bearded Piero Crommelynck, the master printer who worked closely with Picasso during his later years. The artist himself is clearly present in this work — perhaps not surprising for the co-founder of Cubism, whose stylistic experimentation transformed the conventional notion of portraiture and allowed us to view the world from multiple vantage points.

Stephanie Plunkett
Deputy Director/Chief Curator
Norman Rockwell Museum

Roman
Marble bust of a priest
Hadrianic period, AD 117-138
Marble
24.6 x 16.4 x 9.4 inches
Courtesy of The Metropolitan Museum
of Art, Private Collection, New York
(L.2007.8.5)
Image © The Metropolitan Museum of Art

This bust looks more like a Roman statesman or a Roman general ready to go to battle. The eyes have a penetrating look and the nose and mouth are quite distinctive. His facial expression is so serious and somewhat pious, and he appears to be in deep thought.

He has an intimidating, but wise, air. Although his features look familiar, we can say with some confidence that he does not resemble any of our customers. Instead, this portrait reminds us of our grandfather when we were children. Being a first generation immigrant, he was very stern, both in his mannerism and facial expressions. When our grandfather looked at us in this way, we knew he commanded respect.

Dave and Jim Raneri
Proprietors
Charles Department Store

Imperial Roman portraits of private individuals are often extraordinarily nuanced in how they depict office, station, and character. This sensitive marble bust was carved during the Hadrianic period. The sitter wears a rolled fillet that would have included a painted seven-pointed star at its center, an attribute that identifies the elderly man as a priest, possibly of the god Sarapis. As he turns his head to the right he gazes at the viewer with an expression of grave seriousness. He wears a toga passing diagonally across his chest from the left shoulder. His short bangs are combed forward and his sharp, gaunt features are accentuated by wrinkled skin and other signs of advanced age. The tendons of the neck, the hollow cheeks, the thin, pursed lips and hooked nose lend an air of severity with a faint note of weariness.

Michael Bennett
Curator of Greek and Roman Art
The Cleveland Museum of Art

I see ancient eyes on the face of a child. Her eyes are deep pools, pools that reflect generations of women named Sarah, Rebecca, Rachel, and Leah. I see in her eyes their suffering, their strength, and their wisdom.

She looks at us from the shadows. Her face conceals her emotion. I look and I wonder: is she troubled? Is she at peace? Is she resigned to her fate? Her face reflects the faces of other Jewish children of that era: Anne Frank, smiling; the unknown boy walking out of the Warsaw ghetto, his hands raised in surrender. I look at her face and think of the faces of the precious souls whose lights were extinguished in those years of shadow.

This is the face of a child who deserves to live in a world of love and peace and joy, as all children do. May we make it so.

**Jennifer Jaech
Senior Rabbi
Temple Israel of Northern
Westchester
Croton-on-Hudson, NY**

Anne-Karin Furunes creates haunting, large-scale paintings of faces and landscapes by perforating the surface of black or white canvas with thousands of differently sized holes. The holes allow the image to coalesce for the viewer, similar to the halftone images in a newspaper. Furunes's subtly pixelated images of particular people and sites reflect the artist's concern with memory, history, and the nature of photographic reality.

In this series *Portraits of Archive Pictures, 2011*, Furunes draws our attention to children who have lost their individuality and become targeted because of their religion or ethnicity—a tragic reoccurrence throughout history. To illustrate this, Furunes draws upon a photographic archive from Uppsala, Sweden from the 1910s and 1920s, focusing mainly on anonymous Jewish youth who were registered by the government because of their religion. Furunes chooses faces that suggest the presence of a real personality, enigmatic and ungraspable. Rather than explicitly conveying emotion, these faces draw us in, making a connection beyond language and identity.

**Carole Hochman
Director, Barry Friedman Ltd.**

Felix Gonzalez-Torres (1957-1996)
"Untitled" (Portrait of Dad), 1991
White candies individually wrapped in
cellophane, endless supply
Overall dimensions vary with installation
Ideal weight 175 lbs
© The Felix Gonzalez-Torres Foundation
Courtesy of Andrea Rosen
Gallery, New York

When I first look I see a pile of jagged white stones. The room looks quiet and cool. It reminds me of a workroom in a simple home in Greece, where the stones have been swept up and piled, waiting to be used the next day.

But then I see that it's candy! The pile is smaller and certainly sweeter than I had previously thought. But why is the candy on the floor? These mints remind me of Christmas candy—so why are they in a quiet room in Greece?

What a silly thing to do with candy—pile it on the floor. What about ants? And was the floor swept first? I'd only eat the mints on the top of the pile—they'd be cleanest. But I do love these mints...so maybe I'd eat a few more. But would they be dusty? I worry, but I eat them anyway.

Jennifer Cook
Proprietor
NoKa Joe's & Little Joe's Books

What do we see? A pyramid shape comprised of tiny pieces piled on top of one another—what are they made of?

Upon closer inspection we see that this pointed mound is made up of candies, nestled against a wall. The piece is titled *Untitled (Portrait of Dad)*.

It brings back memories of perfectly-formed mountains surrounding deserts in the Southwest region of our country. It suggests sand castles built by young children on a pure white beach. At the same time the mound is frigidly snow-covered, patiently waiting for the first ski patrol to carve tracks. It is a triangle, although far more gentle than any found in a geometry book.

Is this mound representative of the relationship of father and son? The body changes, can it be reinvented? The overall scope of tending and loving and being there for a person is being expressed. Suggested in the wrapped candies are the tiny unsung moments of parenting that go into raising a child. It is a global view and also a microscopic one. The parts rest on each other and belong to each other, as in family relationships.

Feliz Gonzalez-Torres might have asked these questions himself, "Why is this a portrait? How did I form it?" He knows that possibility for change can occur on a kitchen table.

"Start wherever you are. Don't look like anyone else."

Helena Louise Sokoloff
Photographer

Unveiling

I'm veil and word
a cartography that cloaks

mouth and chant
with inky red to black

Farsi songs drone
across my brow

inscribe a code of din
Look, I'm your secret

At dead center my eyes
hide like mirrors

How face is an absence
becoming presence

Look, give my voice a body
give body this voice

**Pamela Hart
Poet**

The first thing I think of when I see this image is the college English class where we debated a quotation that the oppressed know more about the oppressor than the oppressors ever know about the oppressed.

I Am Its Secret portrays a woman in a burka-like head garment, mouth concealed, with knowing eyes, at the center of a spiral with red and black lettering that reminds me of a sacred text (the New Testament has red and black lettering, for instance). To me, she is a silent woman who witnesses everything and understands, in a truly sacred sense, the difference between real wisdom and convenient hierarchies.

And I can't help but root for someone to let the secret out.

**Dar Williams
Singer/Songwriter**

John Singleton Copley (1738-1815)
Mrs. John Scollay (Mercy Greenleaf), 1763
Oil on canvas
35.25 x 28 inches
Driscoll Babcock

I tried to warm up to Mrs. John Scollay. She seemed quite foreboding. I wanted to like her, but she was distant...and perhaps a little defiant. I zeroed in on her maiden name, Mercy Greenleaf, a pretty name for a young woman and the softness in her face was still evident. But as Mrs. Scollay, she seemed tough, masculine, and weary. Could she have been thinking of how hard it was to be a colonist prior to the Revolution? Or was she reflecting on what it meant to be a wife and mother of eleven with an activist husband? As Copley painted her, there seem to be more questions than answers. Perhaps that was his point. A fine portrait needs to tell a story but leave the viewer with enough to ponder. Mrs. Scollay was obviously a force.

Janet Langsam
Chief Executive Officer
ArtsWestchester

Confident, composed, and relaxed. When I look at *Mrs. John Scollay (Mercy Greenleaf)*, she stares right back, not hesitant to meet one's gaze. No shrinking violet or passive object, Scollay inhabits the space with an assured presence befitting the matriarch of a prominent Boston family, whose name was given to the city's Scollay Square. The mother of eleven children and most certainly aware of, if not actively involved in, the growing tensions between colonial America and the British crown, her eyes have the glint of someone who has seen it all. Her luxurious silk dress with intricate lace detailing gives her an added air of royalty. To me, she embodies not only the picture of 18th-century American power, but also a formidable lady by today's standards.

Tess Schwab
Associate Director
Driscoll Babcock Gallery

Russian
Saint Nicholas, ca. 1600
12.375 x 11 x 2 inches
Tempera on panel with gold frame
Private collection, Katonah, NY
Photo: Margaret Fox

We had been collecting icons for some time when we acquired Saint Nicholas. The art form itself represents a way of looking at the unknown and unknowable in two dimensions. The very static quality of the iconography is its appeal, as we can all read into it what we choose. We see it and beyond it simultaneously.

We had been looking for a Saint Nicholas, as our son's name is Nicholas. This particular depiction caught our attention not only for the purity of the painting, but also for the expression of sweetness and wisdom. Saint Nicholas looks at the viewer with compassion and understanding of the human condition. It is no surprise that he has morphed into Santa Claus, the giver of gifts.

Private Collector

I wonder if St. Nicholas were to see this portrait if he would recognize himself.
Halo encircling his head,
Ornate vestments,
Gold backdrop.
I doubt it.

Isn't this the same Nicholas who, on Christmas Eve, went around after dark so as not to be seen giving away so that others would have food enough for one more day?

Maybe we imagine saints as "more" and paint them that way in order that we might hold them at arm's length.

Because if they looked too human;
Too much like you and me;
We would feel more pressure to emulate them rather than just to pray to them.

I wonder if St. Nicholas were to see this portrait if he would recognize himself.
Maybe he would...
But not in the halo or the gold, but in the wrinkled face and the gazing eyes.

Rev. Paul Alcorn
Bedford Presbyterian Church

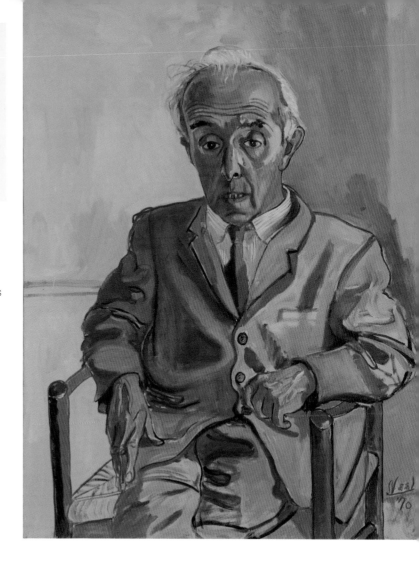

Alice Neel's portraits are not usually tender reflections of their subject matter. Part of Neel's strength as a painter, perhaps even her principal strength, is the raw truth that tends to burst out of her work. The result is that she handles her subject matter with nothing close to kid gloves. How she felt about Raphael Soyer shouts visually from the work: it reeks with tenderness, which is not usually the first thing that comes to mind in observing her work. It is a wonderful example of how well Neel gets her truth down on the canvas.

**William Louis-Dreyfus
Collector**

It took nerve to agree to sit for an Alice Neel portrait. You could not count on flattery. You could expect the slash of paint and shadow that can reveal the grotesque. She exposed the soul, and for some, that can be an unsettling encounter.

Here sits the Social Realist painter Raphael Soyer, subjecting to the gaze of his longtime friend Alice, giving himself up to her savage eye. He is rewarded with tenderness. Neel has chosen to reveal Soyer's warm character through her sensitive paint handling and drawing. Just look at Soyer's hands; these are the hands of an artist, the tools of his trade. It is where Neel focuses us, as well as on the artist's gentle eyes.

Look again. Note the artist's ashcan palette. Is that sadness in Soyer's gaze? It seems that he is shrinking inside that workaday suit. Maybe Neel is saying, in 1970, *"Time has moved on. People don't want what we're still painting. You are an anachronism."*

Or perhaps she is saying this: *"Forget this new, brash crowd.*

We made it through Abstract Expressionism, old friend. We can make it through this."

**Neil Watson
KMA Executive Director
2005 – 2012**

The Moche Man

"Moche es la mano, Nazca es el ojo." Those were the words that came to my mind when I opened my email and saw the image of *Portrait Head of Cut Lip with Large Facial Stripes*. But to my surprise none of those words came to me in English, neither as a feeling nor as a thought. The meaning only came to me when I switched my mode of being to my native language, Spanish. I laughed at myself at that moment and I walked away from him, from "The Moche Man." I resumed my daily duties and I thought—who wants to write the same thing twice, in English and Spanish, when you can do it once? Naïve Miriam went on and made a date with "The Moche Man" for later that evening.

I turned on my computer and I saw him again. I looked at his portrait and his eyes gazed at me, making me dizzy, even uncomfortable. Was he teasing me? Was he provoking me? Who was this Moche Man? Hadn't I seen too many huaco retratos in Lima, Peru, to easily respond to this one? What was special about him besides that cut on his lip, which probably reflected a special time in his life that needed to be recorded in a huaco retrato? Was he an important señor in the Moche culture? It didn't really matter to me at that moment whether he was Señor Moche or a simple Moche man. This *Portrait Head* was there in front of me, speaking to me in my native language, bringing back memories of my country, family, and school. He was a reminder that it is possible to love, feel, and have a unique connection with a person, a moment, and even a piece of art in a target language. The Moche Man was a reminder of how bicultural I had become over the years, how I have assumed a duality. How far in time was it since I learned in school how to differentiate among the art of the many cultures in Ancient Peru? And yet how vivid were those memories and how easily they come to mind when you are presented with an image that transports you back to motherland..."Moche is the hand, and Nazca is the eye."

Miriam Aguilar
Literacy Specialist and
ESL teacher

Moche
Portrait Head Fragment, ca. 400-550 AD
Terracotta
6.75 inches high
Courtesy of Samuel Merrin
The Merrin Gallery
Photo: Stefan Hagen

Moche
Portrait Head of Cut Lip with Large Facial Stripes, ca. 100-800 AD
Terracotta
7.5 inches high
Courtesy of Samuel Merrin
The Merrin Gallery
Photo: Stefan Hagen

The collector came to my office, reached into a box and placed the portrait head on my desk. I was captivated. I was immediately transported in time and came face-to-face with this individual. This true portrait exudes the confidence of someone in a position of power and high society in Moche culture. The cuts on his lip suggest to me that he must have been in a successful battle.

This may have helped cement his position of authority.

As a collector, I was drawn to the high quality of the modeling, color, and intact condition. I have placed this portrait head in my bedroom. At night it can be a little eerie, but I know I am well protected.

Samuel Merrin
Collector

47

Late

I didn't know why
my aunt Sandra was holding
that look of displeasure on her face

until I remembered my promise
to pick her up hours ago
so we could go bowling together.

But what would be the point?
a gaze into her ball
(ok, less than regulation size
and lacking any finger holes)
would show every future score–
she ahead of me by at least a
dozen points.

I'll bet she even foresaw
the glass wings on the butterfly
that recently alighted on her nose.

But the ball is the focus here.
To me it looks like
she could be holding it out like a gift,

a thing of terrible significance,
a little world resting in a cloth,
maybe a baby she just found on
the porch.

Billy Collins
U.S. Poet Laureate

I first became aware of the photographs of Diane Arbus as I stood in line, in 1972, at the Museum of Modern Art. The line from 53rd Street snaked around the block onto Fifth Avenue. Despite the many people, everyone was waiting patiently to view the Arbus exhibition. I had just begun to photograph in 1968, taking my first portrait of my son when he was 18 months old. I, too, used a Rolleiflex camera, as did Arbus.

I remember walking outside in the bright sunlight, stunned and emotionally drained by the photographs I had seen. I remember thinking, as I watched the people in line, so many of them looked like Arbus subjects. Arbus tells stories about the people she chooses. She has said, "A

photograph is a secret about a secret. The more it tells you the less you know."

Her subjects become more important than the picture and more complicated. The intangible something she feels and sees becomes more than what it is. She said, "I think no one else would see what I see unless I photograph them."

Soothsayer Madame Sandra is an example of Arbus's unique ability to include not only her subject, but also the accompanying objects in the photograph that help to tell her story. For example, Madame Sandra's surroundings describe her, from the austere way she holds her crystal ball, the straight-backed chair, the plant,

her glasses, her jewelry, the simple flowered dress, a closet door ajar, to a picture above the chair. All of the objects Diane Arbus selected to be in the photograph help to define Madame Sandra and become the photograph we see.

Claire Yaffa
Photographer

Charlie has been working the security detail in the entrance hall of my home for many years. His watchful presence and stern gaze have intimidated many visitors, much to my delight and that of my children and grandchildren. In order to give Charlie some additional work experience, I've permitted him to take on the security assignment at this exhibition. I look forward to welcoming him home soon.

Sondra Peterson
Collector

When I saw this figure I said, "This looks like me when I retire!" I can see myself still in uniform after 20 years of service in a nice cushy security officer position at a museum, a historic landmark, or even at a beachfront resort.

This officer also reminds me of the beginning of my law enforcement career 12 years ago when I was 21 years old. The light brown shirt with dark brown trim and dark brown pants was my uniform while working at a correctional facility in southwest Florida. This was a great time in my life as I found my career, my future wife, and made life goals for myself that I eventually achieved! I hope that when I retire, I look as thin and as relaxed as the officer depicted here.

Matthew 5:9: "Blessed are the peacemakers: for they shall be called the children of God."

Eddie Ramirez
Mount Kisco Police Officer

Peter Steinhauer (b. 1966)
H'Mong Hoa Minority, Vietnam #96, 2002
Photograph 7/45
22 x 18 inches
Collection of Mona and Ron Schlossberg
© Peter Steinhauer
Photo: Margaret Fox

About seven years ago, my wife Mona and I traveled with the Katonah Museum of Art for an incredible adventure to southeast Asia. We purchased this photograph at a gallery in Hanoi—it was on the last day of our two-week trip. When photographer Helena Sokoloff, who was traveling with us, went to purchase this image, Mona got right in line behind her. The photograph is displayed in our front hallway and every time I look at it, I am reminded of that stupendous day.

Ron Schlossberg
Collector

This portrait of a H'mong woman is reminiscent of Edward Curtis's project that documented the Native American way of life before it disappeared. This image portrays a traditional Vietnamese dress and hairstyle soon to be forgotten. The less-than-cheerful expression on the subject's face gives the viewer a foreboding sense. Or you could say she is expressionless, which is typical of a classic portrait.

The photograph is taken with a large-format camera that uses sheet film as revealed in the black borders made by film holders. A portrait lens creates the shallow depth of field and the use of black-and-white film is indicative of a documentary style.

Margaret Fox
Photographer

Red Grooms (b. 1937)
Mondrian, 1990
Painted bronze
24 x 19 x 14.75 inches
Louis-Dreyfus Family Collection
© 2013 Red Grooms/Artists Rights
Society (ARS), New York

Mondrian

Tell us in a brush stroke,
speak the truth
with words not spoken.
Show us in your eyes
the map of the world
in bars and lines.
Everything can be broken
down
into geometry
even what we can't see:
the abstract
becomes reality.
We reside
in the intersections
where time and space
collide.
We are confined
by rigid right angles.
To keep our lives
untangled,
we contain chaos

with borders,
but order
keeps mayhem hidden
from scrutiny.
We construct grids;
we rid
what we can't
define,
we simplify
until patterns
take hold
and new
matches old,
but the truth
will unfold
in the gaps
that can't
be filled.

Callie Deitrick
Student, Hamilton College

What strikes me most about Red Grooms's bronze sculpture of Piet Mondrian is the total absence of any emotion. It doesn't really surprise me that Mondrian, the artist of geometry, would be seen as having nary a flicker of emotion in his face, or one might say, jailed by his own structure as shown in the portrait.

In my opinion, this portrait represents the opposite of what I feel is the point of a portrait—creating an emotional reaction in the viewer. The paintings of Mondrian make me feel distant and flat.

In most cases, an artist painting a portrait hopes to find a way for the viewer to feel a connection to the subject, be it identification, revulsion, sadness, or beauty. A portrait aims to communicate a viewpoint, which the artist wants to convey.

Samuel Klagsbrun, MD
Executive Medical Director
Four Winds Hospital

51

ALIEN ENTITEES WHO HAVE BEEN SEEN VISITING OUR PLANET

KG06

Ken Grimes (b. 1947)
Untitled (Alien entities), 2006
Acrylic on panel
48 x 72 inches
Private collection
Photo: Margaret Fox

Ken Grimes's exploration of the relationship of extra-terrestrials and their cultures to our civilization has often struck me as a challenge to humans to broaden views of themselves. The artist asks us to re-evaluate and begin to re-orient our perspectives. He has a wonderful sense of humor and, in this work, Grimes's directness and sincerity give it an engaging and zany quality. Each 'visitor' has a quirky personality. I always think of them as alien tourists. It hangs in our family room.

Private Collector

Symbols have been used by people since the dawn of human expression. Symbols codify and solidify thoughts and meaning. At first look, Ken Grimes's *Untitled (Alien entities)* reads like a cartoon, but further observation reveals something more sinister—a wanted poster for the uninvited. The "other."

Each of Grimes's aliens shares common traits: head, eyes, and mouth. They are like us, but not just like us. They are different enough to warrant our suspicion. The negative space around each character seems to place each portrait in a dark void. We would like to imagine that we would be unafraid when encountering someone or something we do not fully understand, but our history and our past tell us that this is not the case. Aliens are different. Aliens are not us. They belong on wanted posters.

Spencer Eldridge
Art Teacher
John Jay Middle School

Even without the title, you know this portrait depicts an important Tibetan lama because he has a golden halo studded with wish-fulfilling jewels and he is seated on an ornately carved and painted wooden throne, one that has gold and red brocades draped over the back and golden dragons holding wish-fulfilling jewels as crossbar-ends. He is swathed in layers of sumptuous robes (it's cold in Tibet) and he wears the hat of an Indian scholar. Above him are teachers that came before him in his lineage and below are protective deities.

This lama's facial features may seem stylized at first, but the slight squint of his eyes and his upturned mouth suggest an intelligent and personable disposition. His rounded cheeks, double chin, and long white beard distinguish him from other abbots of Ngor Monastery, who are depicted making the same gesture of teaching and with the same hat and halo. The small table in front of him is set with ritual objects, including a smoking incense burner on the left.

**Kathryn Selig Brown
Curator**

Whenever I look at a painting of a face, I think of my mother, who has painted portraits for 60 years. When I posed for her as a child, I always wondered what she thought about while she painted and why a person would paint a picture of another person's face. Later I came to think of painting as an incredibly unique way of representing reality and time—painting suggests an interpretation of a person and a life. The act of painting and paintings themselves fascinate me.

This beautiful thangka painting reminds me of living in India and visiting Tibet in 1994. My senses were on overload. I was beginning to learn a bit about Tibetan Buddhism and its focus on the way that the mind works—how mind influences the way we visualize and interpret everything.

What's interesting about this painting is that it gives more than a momentary glimpse of the subject. The beautiful scenes, aspects of nature, and beings that surround the abbot offer timelessness—details about the abbot's past, his life, his reality and dreams.

However, despite all the adornments, distractions, and details in this painting, my eye keeps coming back to the serene, gentle, and kind expression on the abbot's face. This face embodies the world.

**Vanessa H. Smith
Filmmaker**

Joseph Hardin (1921-1989)
Marilyn Monroe, 1989
Paint on poster board
10 x 14 inches
Collection of Audrey B. Heckler
Photo: Margaret Fox

In spite of being severely crippled with arthritis, Outsider artist Joseph Hardin shows no hesitation or pretense in making his art. Raw, uncensored, pure creativity. Powerful strokes define the essence of Marilyn Monroe. Eyes with long lashes, bright red lips, predominant breasts, and colored nail polish all convey the exuberant Miss Monroe.

**Mary Lou Alpert
Art Curator**

Joseph Hardin suffered from rheumatoid arthritis, a crippling disease that confined him to a wheelchair from the age of seven. Although his hands could hardly hold a paint brush, he painted to create a whole world for himself, wallpapering his room with his artwork. He especially loved women, and because he couldn't have them, he drew them. His women were the objects of his sexual desire, his fantasies, and were usually depicted nude with big boobs and foreshortened limbs.

I have two paintings by Hardin, *Marilyn Monroe* and *Woman with a Blue Dog*. I love them because they stand out—they're vivid, bold, and in-your-face.

**Audrey Heckler
Collector**

Edward Curtis (1868-1952)
Nalin, Apache Portrait, 1903
Photogravure
17 x 13 inches
Collection of Steven and
Nevine Michaan
Photo: Margaret Fox

I was just 20 years old, a college student at Berkeley, when I purchased *Nalin* at a gallery in California. It has remained a personal favorite of mine throughout many decades of collecting. The portrait has always been prominently displayed in our home; for years it was above my desk, now it hangs in our front foyer. It is a piece I will always keep. Also, it is one of the few artworks that my wife likes too.

Steven Michaan
Collector

N alin has such a clear, distinct connection with me—no hesitation or shyness, just a deep self-possessed exchange. She reminds me that it is important to be recognized in a real way. Thanks to the prodigious efforts of Edward Curtis, we have remarkable documentation of Native American lives, languages, and customs predating the humiliation that came from failed treaties and government efforts at civilization. He photographed with dignity, truth, and artistry.

For me, Nalin's direct gaze brings to mind events that were impressionable. In 1964 my husband and I participated in planning a national Girl Scout Roundup in Northern Idaho for 12,000 scouts. The other organizers were prominent men who were less than interested in having Indians involved. Despite my initial timidity, I stood and suggested that Indians must be represented. The basis of my courage was the Indian art of the Northwest I had seen. Indeed, the encampment in 1965 included a major forum "The American Indian Yesterday, Today, and Tomorrow" with an exhibition of Nez Perce tribal artifacts. Tribe members came, danced, and shared food—a profound experience for all.

Inge Brown
KMA Founder

Lincoln Schatz (b. 1963)
Portrait of Jeff Bezos from the series,
Esquire's Portrait of the 21st Century,
2008
Generative video work, Mac Mini
computer, custom software,
display monitor
Courtesy of the artist

"The bastard form of mass culture is humiliated repetition… always new books, new programs, new films, news items, but always the same meaning."
—Roland Barthes

Lincoln Schatz's *Portrait of Jeff Bezos* captures the man who gave us the electronic book and plays on this sense of repetition in a voyeuristic gaze—yet moves beyond Barthes' characterization of mass culture. Bezos is self-conscious in a way that we have all become in a world of cameras marking our way through daily life. Schatz captures the mundane, layering images in a way that evokes our sense of screens and cameras as appendages. Bezos sits, imprisoned in his cube, captured by video surveillance staring at his screen as we stare at him on ours—the layers of light and image playing on us in a way that transcends literal meaning.

**Stephen Apkon
Founder and Executive Director
Jacob Burns Film Center**

My first thought while watching this was: "figures he would bring in the Kindle!" Jeff Bezos has already completely changed the world, and yet he wants to do it again through the Kindle, so of course he would insist this be a part of the portrait. In this way, Jeff's portrait shows Jeff for who he is—a personification of the "Silicon Valley ethos." By which I mean, the leaders of the technology revolution—Bezos, Brin and Page, Jobs—they all share a few personality traits that are evident in this portrait.

First, a casual approach to the world. Jeff is wearing jeans (as usual), relaxing in a chair. Second, unbelievable amounts of energy. Jeff cannot sit still. None of them can, physically or metaphorically. Third, a strong belief that they know what everyone wants. This is why I think he included the Kindle. He knows that it will change the world. It's his legacy. How could he possibly not have it with him?

Bezos could completely rest on his laurels. Amazon has changed the face of commerce forever. It's a household name. And yet, he and his company have other windmills to tilt at, whether it is cloud computing (most people outside the industry don't know that they are the biggest player in this space), or how we consume information.

And yet, what has always amazed me is that when you meet these titans, they're just regular guys, in jeans, twirling in a chair.

**Jeremy Sussman, PhD
Google**

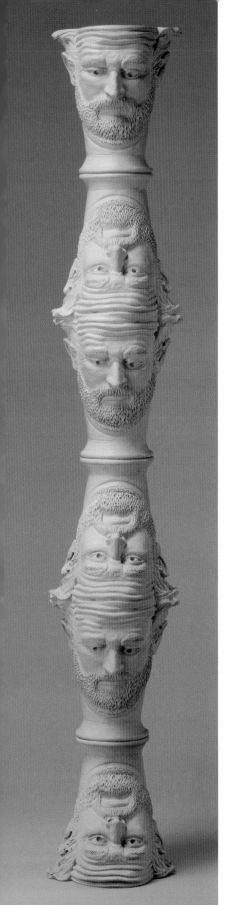

Premise: Six men waiting on line at a local post office

Man 1 *(4:05pm)* How many window clerks can be on a break at the same time?

Man 2 *(4:15pm)* If I put a mirror under those clerks noses will it eventually steam up?

Man 3 *(4:30pm)* If I've gotten the wrong mail in my mailbox do you think someone got my mail? (Clerk: DUH...)

Man 4 *(4:40pm)* If I sent a package with tracking and it never arrived can we still find it? (Clerk: If it's lost, it's lost)

Man 5 *(4:50pm)* My wife got on this line when she was eight-months pregnant. She left and now we have a one-month-old girl.

Man 6 *(4:59pm)* I've been on line since 4:00 pm. Can I still mail it? (Clerk: Sorry sir, we're closed)

Anonymous Postal Clerk

Robert Arneson references Constantin Brâncuși's *Endless Column*, also an exploration of the infinite; both have no beginning or end. Each welcomes never-ending interpretations that the contemplation of art invites. But Arneson gets right to the point—people, especially artists, are infinitely self-focused. Brâncuși's pillar universally contemplates life. Arneson's totem-like self-portrait explicitly suggests we are at our best when self-reflective capacities are practiced.

As with most of Arneson's work, his humor is in praise of folly, that is, he often deals with serious issues—the best jokes do. And the truly funny gags focus on the comedian, giving audiences the opportunity to have a secure gut-wrenching laugh even when the joke is on us. Arneson's endless self-meditative column, completed the same year he died, instructs about eternity, but he has left us with himself. Again Arneson has the last laugh. Ha ha.

Rev. Dr. Paul S. Briggs
Antioch Baptist Church

My first reaction is an unspoken conversation between a couple getting ready for the day. The inquisitive look on the man's face as he finishes dressing suggests, "Are you really going to wear that?" The look on the woman's face suggests, "I really don't care what you think, I like my bracelet!"

Casey Carter
Owner
Bijou Fine Jewelry, Katonah, NY

*T*he Krakoffs are entangled in contrasts and ambiguity.

The couple unite and divide in the central black swath.

Her arm and face confront us from this void, the uncertainty of her expression compounded by the up-and-down curve of her lips. He breathes in the shallow space behind—the messy real world of grimaces, unshaven faces, wrinkled brows, double chins, and going through the motions.

His black arm tears the corner of the pure white square of the wall beyond. She is pinned to her quadrant of the painting.

He directs us to the imperfections of form and color in the (lamp) light of reality, disdaining her simplistic dichotomy of a black and white relationship.

He twists into the baroque. She rests in the classical.

His space is layered. Her world is flat.

His arm is a clock hand. Her arm rests.

He is engaged. She is divorced.

Barbara Lowenthal
Architect

Martine Franck (1938-2012)
Portrait of Henri Cartier-Bresson, 1992
Modern gelatin silver print
16 x 20 inches
Collection of Ellen and Robert Grimes
Courtesy Magnum Photos

My husband and I had begun to form a collection of French photographers and we wanted an image by Henri Cartier-Bresson to complete our grouping. We knew well his iconic work and wanted something less "knee-jerk" Cartier-Bresson. I saw this print at a photography fair and loved how it captures (1) Cartier-Bresson's image of himself, (2) Martine Franck's image of her husband, and (3) the viewer's ability to see both perspectives. To get three points of view of the same subject captured in one photograph was tremendously appealing. So while this wasn't an image by Cartier-Bresson, it was of him in a unique way. Flexibility kicked in and we very happily added it to our group.

Ellen Grimes
Collector

A *pas de deux*—a dance for two persons—might seem an inappropriate metaphor for a photographic portrait of a man at work, but here, the viewer beholds a seamless expression of two artists' visions. Intertwining gazes of artist and subject heighten the intensity of the portrait, and the viewer is invited to observe this dynamic but not fully participate. Artfully framed by the window, the reflection in the mirror, the self-portrait the man renders, and the wintry urban landscape wholly engage the viewer. The photographer's gaze, however— seen only by the man in the mirror's reflection—remains inaccessible to others who are still privileged to see the lost profile of a man engrossed in his own creativity. One artist documents another at work, crafting an artifice that allows access only to the dancers' creative process, while excluding the viewer from the most intimate artistic dialogue.

Amy Herman
Director
The Art of Perception

Cindy Sherman (b. 1954)
Untitled (MP #473), 2008
Color photograph
Edition 1/6
70.25 x 60 inches
© Cindy Sherman
Courtesy of the artist and Metro Pictures,
New York

Sadness. Insecurity. Money doesn't buy you happiness—or beauty for that matter. These are my first impressions when I look at Cindy Sherman's 'Socialite' image. Let me explain. The fur. The jewelry. The over-the-top makeup. She looks like so many women of a certain age with a certain bank account trying to use money to impress. But instead of looking beautiful, I think she looks pained by the burden of trying too hard.

I want to say to this woman, "Less is more. Age gracefully. A little makeup goes a long way." Once she takes off the mask and makes peace with herself and her age, her inner beauty will show.

**Andrea Pomerantz Lustig
Author,** *How to Look Expensive:
A Beauty Editor's Secrets to
Getting Gorgeous without
Breaking the Bank*

A portrait of Cindy Sherman is never a self-portrait, but rather a façade. The artist takes on the attributes of various characters, drawing us into cultural masquerades. Here she is featured in the guise of a society matron. Furs and jewels, attributes of wealth, like the scrim of too much make-up, suggest the long tradition of *vanitas* themes in art. Earthly treasures and exercises in vanity cannot protect us from the inevitability of time passing.

The visage of comfort and success is rendered on a scale consistent with the aristocratic portraits of earlier centuries. But the camera's blazing gaze has a cruel and unyielding effect, drawing attention to the sitter's imperfections and the pathos of fading beauty. The background, which seems to be shot elsewhere or added digitally, recalls studio photographs of an earlier age, perhaps even the time when the sitter was in her prime.

**Susan Edwards, PhD
KMA Executive Director
1998 – 2004**

Auguste Rodin (1840-1917)
Mask of Madame Rodin (Rose Beuret)
1880-82
Bronze
10.375 x 6.875 x 5.875 inches
Private collection
Photo: Margaret Fox

One frequently feels the artist's own hand in Auguste Rodin's sculptures, especially his work in clay. One sees the clay shift in many different directions, feels his sense of play with the material, and senses the energy of him sculpting in time.

It is interesting that this unique approach applies to a loved one. Why did it take Rodin two full years to complete this small sculpture?

Were his feelings toward his mistress constantly evolving over time, and thus changing his impression of the sculpture? Or perhaps he felt something very deep toward her and was compelled to continue working on the sculpture until it properly transmitted his feelings about her.

Loren Eiferman
Artist

We are all familiar with the noted artist Auguste Rodin. His famous figural depictions of the human body—brimming with strength, tension, and movement—are mostly cast in dark shimmering bronzes. While this is a sculpture that is meant to be seen in three dimensions, my reaction is exclusively from a frontal point of view. Had I not been approached to write about this sculpture by artist's name, I would have certainly guessed it was created by the hands of the famous sculptor because of its gestural handling of the material, its emotional certitude, and famous patina. Rodin's art is unmistakably his own. With the foot of the neck suggesting other parts of the body, the serious, almost unhappy expression, the hair up to reveal the entire contours of her head, the sitter gives the viewer the impression of not being amused by having to pose for this rendering. Had the rest of her body been included it would certainly express the same kind of emotion as that on her face.

George King
KMA Executive Director
1988 – 1998

Chinese
Ancestor Portrait, ca. 1860
57.5 x 37.5 inches
Ink and mineral colors on tightly woven
silk, mounted on paper
Lisbeth and Frank Stern
Photo: Margaret Fox

Our gazes meet across centuries, from your ancient past to my present. What has the artist conveyed across time? Eyes with a clear and penetrating gaze. Calmness emanates from you. Your deep blue robes flow into fields of flowers. Are they chrysanthemums—a flower of beauty, hardship, and fortitude? What have you endured in your long life—love, success, tragedy, disappointments? A venerable age has brought you to this pinnacle of wisdom. You sit on your chair, feet square on the earth, stable in your power and veneration. Did you know that you would be immortal?

Diane Moller
Library Media Specialist
Lewisboro Elementary School

We came across this gentle-looking portrait as we wandered through the antique district in Hong Kong on Hollywood Road twenty years ago. We were struck by the expression on the man's face, so much like our grandfathers.

These portraits, referred to as "ancestor paintings," were specifically painted for use in ancestor worship. The face was the most important part of the portrait, and therefore, artists went to great lengths to make it as realistic as possible.

Sadly, once photography was developed, the demand for such portraits declined. Much of Chinese culture and history is revealed in these paintings, and somehow they speak to us in a way that photographs can never equal.

Lisbeth and Frank Stern
Collectors

Käthe Kollwitz (1867-1945)
Self-Portrait, 1921
Etching on cream Japan paper
Signed lower right
8.75 x 10.5 inches
Courtesy Galerie St. Etienne, New York

Like many of the German and Austrian Expressionists (Max Beckmann, Lovis Corinth, Egon Schiele), Käthe Kollwitz is renowned for her self-portraits. These works are not so much affirmations of self as explorations of personal identity. Perhaps because, as a woman, Kollwitz faced many professional obstacles, she was haunted by self-doubt. Her 1921 self-portrait captures the relentless process of questioning, introspection, and perseverance that shaped her entire career. I chose this image for the invitation of one of the first exhibitions I ever curated, in the early 1980s, because I found it especially moving. I still do.

Jane Kallir
Director
Galerie St. Etienne

This self-portrait immediately made me wonder why this middle-aged artist appeared to be so lost in serious and deep thought. Lacking any sign of beauty or femininity, at first I thought, incorrectly, that the artist was a male. But as her name might suggest, Käthe is a sensitive and bright woman who has seen much in her life. She is wondering what else lies ahead for her. She has experienced much sadness, perhaps the loss of loved ones, and she is trying to make sense of her life. It may be an existential moment for her—a time of asking why her life has taken the turns it has, a time of searching for answers, answers that probably aren't there.

Joel Seligman
President
Northern Westchester Hospital

Robert Henri (1865-1929)
Portrait of Marcia Ann M. Tucker, 1926
Oil on canvas
60 x 40.5 inches
Driscoll Babcock

Aunt Marcia I knew her as, but she wasn't Aunt Marcia then. The booze and cancer and cigarettes and multiple husbands were still years in her future. She was a beautiful child of the twenties—the decade we call roaring—exquisite to behold, rich, a party animal. She drove her strait-laced mother nuts. She was trouble with a capital T and effervescent and demanding.

You can see it in the portrait, can't you? The beauty, the strong gaze, the steely determination to defy her steely mama (emphasis on the second syllable—ma*ma*). An anarchic fearlessness—the privilege (or curse) of great wealth.

She died sad—in her forties—but that was later. Is Robert Henri hinting at her fate in her haunting gaze, or knowing her history am I reading backwards?

Carll Tucker
Publisher and Editor

Robert Henri's *Portrait of Marcia Ann M. Tucker* depicts a girl on the cusp of womanhood whose confidence is suggested in the casual nature of her pose and the direct gaze at the artist. Her youthful, innocent appearance is belied by the book that she cradles in her lap, seemingly interrupted in her pursuit of knowledge. She may be beautiful, but she prefers to present herself as an unconventional modern young woman who will embrace the opportunities that are presented.

Henri emphasizes the "action" within the pose by surrounding the girl's head with dark tones and picking up the white tights against the dark background to direct the viewer's eye towards the center of attention, thus avoiding a static composition. The action is balanced by the red cloth, which drapes vertically on the arm of the chair to create a feeling of tranquility. The simplicity of the clothing and the hairstyle provide few clues to the precise time period of this painting.

Wende Caporale
Artist

Sperandio
Federigo da Montefeltro (1422-1482)
25
Bronze, cast
Diameter 89.5 mm (3.52 inches)
Courtesy of Frances Beatty and
Allen Adler

Matteo de' Pasti
Isotta degli Atti of Rimini
(born 1432/33, died 1474)
12
Bronze alloy, cast
Diameter 85.20 mm (3.35 inches)
Courtesy of Frances Beatty and
Allen Adler

While Matteo de' Pasti is documented as a manuscript illuminator, painter, and architect, his surviving figural works are portrait medals. Most relate to his role as artist and counselor to the Malatesta court in Rimini.

The portrait medal was still a novel art form when Sigismondo Malatesta adopted it to honor himself and his beloved, Isotta degli Atti. The beautiful daughter of a Riminese merchant had inspired his passion when she was barely thirteen years old. The date 1446 commemorates the triumphal year when Sigismondo consolidated his political power, dedicated his new castle, and won Isotta as his mistress. Besides proclaiming his love, the medal exalted the cultural glamor of the Rimini court.

Sperandio of Mantua is known primarily as a medallist, although he was also active as a goldsmith, painter, sculptor, architect, and cannon founder. While living in Bologna, Sperandio completed a large number of medals, including this one of Federigo da Montefeltro, Duke of Urbino.

A *condottiere* of remarkable ability, Federigo da Montefeltro enjoyed an extraordinary reputation, both during his lifetime and after his death, for his military sagacity, his scholarly devotion, and his just rule of Urbino. Federigo was held in high esteem by his contemporaries both at home and abroad. Sperandio's portrait shows the duke in old age, in an image containing the weight of his experience and reputation. In deliberate imitation of the posthumous deification of Roman emperors, the word DIVI is included in the inscription.

Frances Beatty and Allen Adler
Collectors

These medals are emblematic of two very different facets of the public image Renaissance nobility sought to cultivate. On one medal, we see the face of a hardened military veteran, his grim and unsmiling face pictured from the left so as to hide the scars and disfigurement he had suffered.

The back side shows him with sword in hand, charging into battle atop his horse, reminding the medal's beholder that this duke was a man of violence, a leader skilled in the art of war.

The other medal displays an altogether different sort of figure. Minted by a lord to honor a mistress he clearly cared for, this medal displays her in all her beauty, clothed in fine garments. The elephant on the back ties her symbolically to a famous empress and shows us that at least some noblemen of the time placed as much stock in those they loved as others did in their accomplishments on the battlefield.

Marcus Hausler
Student, Vassar College

Stettheimer Paints Duchamp

Florine Stettheimer (1871–1944)
Marcel Duchamp, 1923
Oil on canvas
30 x 26 inches
Private collection of
William Kelly Simpson

Elevation of eccentric identity only
works if it's effortless.
A nonchalance whispering poems
about the painter.
The self, self-conscious work of
calculated art.
The artist sees an artist bit by
bit—a portrait inside out.

A nonchalance whispering poems
about the painter.
C'est la vie, Marcel—Florine puts
lightness on the palette.
The artist sees an artist bit by
bit—a portrait inside out.
Red is never without meaning
[blushing pink].

C'est la vie, Marcel—Florine puts
lightness on the palette.
DM, DM, DM—a drum roll and
she's floating on a wire.
Red is never without meaning
[blushing pink].
Impatient Time must always have
a window.

DM, DM, DM—a drum roll and
she's floating on a wire.
The chair, the crossed legs, chess
moves—all just so.
Impatient Time must always have
a window.
She knows we are all ephemeral, at
best ethereal.

The chair, the crossed legs, chess
moves—all just so.
The self, self-conscious work of
calculated art.
She knows we are all ephemeral, at
best ethereal.
Elevation of eccentric identity only
works if it's effortless.

Laura Vookles
Chief Curator of Collections
Hudson River Museum

Florine Stettheimer's painting of Marcel Duchamp brings to mind a psychiatrist's office. The psychiatrist and the patient are pictured during one of their sessions. The clock in the middle of the painting reminds me of the confinements of time in which a psychotherapy session takes place. The female patient, wearing a pink dress, dominates the scene. She expresses herself verbally during the session while she gestures openly and confidently with her right hand. She also sits on her left hand and crosses her right foot behind her leg, indicative of some self-reservation. The dark shadow outside the open window may represent the patient's illness that appears ambiguous and potentially frightening, and visible only to the patient in this scene.

The psychiatrist appears focused and an active participant in the session, although he is not speaking. The window remains hidden from the psychiatrist's view, perhaps meaning that the patient has not yet discussed this aspect of her life. The psychiatrist is pictured turning a mechanism that links him directly to his patient. His therapeutic touch is gentle and hidden, but effective, as he carefully and thoughtfully works to lift his patient, guiding her closer to the important elements of her illness.

Jessica Nowillo, DO
Psychiatrist

Christopher French (b. 1957)
Vital Statistics CY, 1998
Oil on chromogenic photographic paper
mounted on wood panel
24 x 18 inches
Courtesy of the artist

This work marries the more than one method of communication and identification to illustrate who we are. While the fingerprint is a relatively contemporary method of identification, it has existed as long as man himself and is uniquely individual. The Braille descriptors within the print seem to represent what cannot be "seen" by all but still lies within the individual.

William J. Hayes
Chief of Police
Bedford Police Department

A Circle of Life

I am looking straight down at a cross-section of a trunk that was once a mighty vibrant tree. Ancient growth rings sputter from a center core in a rhythmic pattern of concentric circles like electron valence shells orbiting in perpetuity, confined only by the diameter of the trunk itself.

Colorations across its bandwidth are reminders that nature's elements had very much been at play—the ebb and flow of moisture and heat have left a muted browning against a darkened palate of growth rings. The pith is riddled with perfectly pock-marked divots, evidence that perhaps life was also extended to a host of burrowing insects that once took sanctuary there.

What I take from Christopher French's work is that we are not only commemorating a cross-section of life, but its growth and decay as well, for this is as natural and as integral as life itself. Each ring symbolizes a ladder to our continuous development and evolution, but ultimately and inevitably becomes life's ending point for all of us.

Anthony Himmel
Senior Claims Officer
NYC Law Department

Kitagawa Utamaro (c. 1753-1806)
Renowned Beauties Likened to the Six Immortal Poets: Appearing again, the Teahouse Waitress Naniwaya Okita
ca. 1795-6
Woodblock print
14.625 x 9.875 inches
Scholten Japanese Art, New York

Images of beautiful women in Japanese art are called *bijin-ga* (lit. 'beautiful person picture'). Prints or paintings of this era depicted famous courtesans and entertainers in order to display the latest fashions in kimono fabrics and hairstyles. While most *bijin-ga* represented an idealized beauty, this print is actually a portrait of a specific beauty, albeit a highly stylized interpretation by the artist. Okita was a waitress who worked at the Naniwaya teahouse near the Asakusa Temple in Edo (Tokyo). At the time this print was made, she would have been only seventeen years old. What makes this print so interesting is that it is a portrait of a real person who we can identify, even though she was 'only' a tea house waitress. Okita's beauty and grace transcended her station in life, bringing her to the attention of the great artist Utamaro, who was so taken with her that he depicted her in over thirty prints and paintings during his lifetime. And now, here she hangs on a museum wall...allowing her to transcend time as well.

Katherine Martin
Director
Scholten Japanese Art

Kitagawa Utamaro made a number of prints depicting the young beauty Okita, a teenaged waitress at the Naniwaya teahouse. By the time this print was made, Utamaro had already become a central figure in the artistic world of Edo (old Tokyo) and was being highly praised for his sensual and elegant okubi-e (big head) portraits of women. Here Okita is presenting a lacquer tray on which sits a cup of tea. Her whole demeanor is delicate in the way she holds the tray with her head tipped forward just slightly. Her hair is done up elaborately and held with wooden hair pins.

The artist's signature is printed vertically on the left side above the tea cup and below the hairpins. It translates as "brush of Utamaro." Utamaro had nearly 60 publishers marketing his work. Here the publisher's seal is on the rectangle at the lower left. It reads "hon omiya" (genuine omiya). Just as we use posters and photographs as decorations and souvenirs, so did everyday Japanese enjoy prints, and without publishers the entire field would not have existed.

The production of these prints was a collaborative effort, rather different from most printmaking in the West with individual specialists taking the roles of designer (Utamaro), carver, printer, and publisher. They collaborated to create the supremely high-quality prints that continue to provide us with interest and pleasure today.

Anthony Kirk
Master Printer

American school
Mary Elizabeth Knickerbacker
19th century
Oil on canvas
27 x 23 inches
Private collection of
William Kelly Simpson
Photo: Margaret Fox

I found these portraits quite intriguing. What lasting impression did Joseph and Mary Elizabeth Knickerbacker want to make on the viewer? What aspects of their individual temperaments and characters did they want the painter to capture?

What I perceive when I look at the paintings are handsome, stylish siblings. He makes quite a statement with his dashing coiffure and cravat. Her sartorial choices are striking with exquisite lace, prominent earrings, and a rousing red wrap.

What is going on behind the style-strong personalities? His eyes exude intensity; his gaze radiates a passion and his mouth resoluteness. She emanates calm and looks out with confidence and intelligence. The book in her hand reinforces this perception. Was Mary Elizabeth the steadying calm to Joseph's more passionate nature? Whatever their personal dynamic, they were undoubtedly a captivating and formidable pair.

Heather Langham
President
Friends of John Jay Homestead

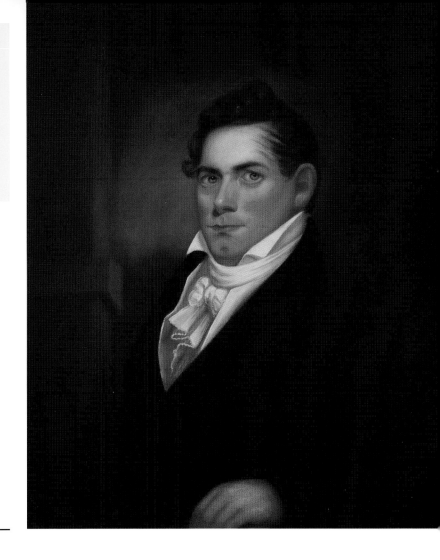

American school
Joseph Foster Knickerbacker
19th century
Oil on canvas
27 x 23 inches
Private collection of
William Kelly Simpson
Photo: Margaret Fox

These two portraits, painted by an unknown artist about 1846, are of a brother and sister from the town of Schaghticoke in Rensselaer County, New York. The young man in the painting, Joseph Foster Knickerbacker (1824-1882), was the son of Abraham Knickerbacker (1796-1869), a wealthy landowner and one of the descendants of the Dutch immigrants who first settled in this small farming and industrial town near Albany. After his wife died in 1825, Abraham married Mary Ann, who subsequently gave birth to their only daughter, Mary Elizabeth Knickerbacker (1830-1846), who is the female depicted in the painting.

Being among the children of one of the most affluent families in town may explain the expensive clothing both are wearing. Or did the artist simply lend costumes to his subjects while they were posing? Why is the young lady, who died at age sixteen, depicted as someone much older and sophisticated than her tender age? Her epitaph in the Schaghticoke cemetery reads "How many hopes lie buried here."

Their last name was a variation of Knickerbocker, memorialized by Washington Irving in his *Knickerbocker's History of New York,* and lives on today with the New York Knicks, who had as their original logo a Dutchman, (Knickerbocker), dribbling a basketball.

Kenneth T. Jackson
Jacques Barzun Professor in
History and the Social Sciences
Columbia University

Chuck Close (b. 1940)
Emma, 2002
113-color hand-printed ukiyo-e
woodcut Edition of 55
36 x 30 inches
Private collection
© Chuck Close, courtesy Pace Gallery

*E*mma captures the innocence of childhood...of being healthy and happy and not knowing life any other way. She seems curious and thoroughly mesmerized by the world surrounding her. Staring at her makes me yearn for the carefree days of my own childhood and it reminds me of precious memories that I have of our children when they were Emma's age.

Sandy Samberg
Founder
Sole Ryeders & Friends

I LOVE Emma. She is so colorful and fun! When you look at her she looks excited and happy. Emma's eyes look like clovers, four-leafed ones. That's why I think she is lucky, and they are as light as the water. And I love the technique with triangles, squares, and circles! She has lots of different COLORS! I think she is beautiful!

Cate Roth
Age 7

72

It is only fitting that Jonathan Becker's brilliantly composed photograph of the SNL cast was taken at Elaine's. Throughout its history, Elaine's was at the center of the literary and artistic nightlife in New York City. This was especially the case in the 1970s when regulars as diverse as Woody Allen and George Plimpton had their own tables. The setting of this image in the kitchen—the cast sharing the scene with a bin of dirty dishes—may have been a wry commentary on the raunchy humor that SNL brought to network TV.

An interesting side note: it was Elaine herself who actually encouraged Becker to become a photographer by setting up an internship for him with the great Hungarian photographer Brassaï, who was a regular at the restaurant whenever he was in New York.

Charles Johnstone
Photographer

I remember first watching *Saturday Night Live* and thinking that it was a revelation. Someone, some group of people, had the same sense of humor that I did and they were voicing it on national television! It was a revolution, a changing of the guard, it was the first popular cultural phenomenon that my slice of generation could claim: not quite flower child, not quite disco, waiting for the change to come.

The photo at Elaine's is visceral on many levels. Out Plimpton! Out Wolfe! Out Talese! Make way for these guys! Irreverent guys, but clearly happy to be there in that place. Elaine's place. That messy place. Those messy guys.

Looking into the past, one wonders what Lorne had in his briefcase. If Elaine's was still in business, would he now be the one at the tables, readers low on his nose, looking at the ruckus in the kitchen? Out Aykroyd! Out Chase! Certainly, out Belushi. The question is, who, now, is in the kitchen?

Steel Swift
President
Tangram International Exhibitions

Annie Oakley's character was as colorful as this silkscreen. I sense determination in her eyes, seriousness in her facial expression, and a strong sense of pride in her stature. Her gaze is fixed at a distance, perhaps on her next target, or perhaps on the goal of equity for women—not just at the shooting range. Her medals communicate accomplishment, though we know they fail to recognize some of her greatest contributions, which were charitable, philanthropic, and truly historic. It's not hard to imagine that Annie was a pioneer of women's equality when viewing this work of art.

Congresswoman Nita M. Lowey representing New York's 17th Congressional District

The portrait looks just like I would have envisioned Annie Oakley because of her cowboy hat, medals, and proud manner.
She looks curious.
She looks like she is interested in something beyond the picture, thoughtful.
She looks like she is very strong.
She looks extremely confident and calm.
My name is Annie, too, and I know most of the songs from "Annie Get Your Gun."
So I know her medals come from being a famous marksman who entertained, showing off her amazing skill all around the world.
She married Frank Butler who was the cowboy who sang the song, "I Can Do Anything You Can Do," with her. And she could do anything any man could do.

Annie Reiner
Age 16

Makusi Panqutu (1933-1973)
Inuit Mother with Twins, ca. 1960
Grey stone
15 x 14 x 12 inches
Arctic Artistry Gallery
Photo: Margaret Fox

My first reaction when looking at this piece was that I wanted to touch it! While carved from stone, the curved lines of this woman's body almost make it look soft. She appears to be a strong, loving mother who would stop at nothing to protect her children. Her arms are protectively wrapped around one child as she feeds him, while the other child is swaddled on her back. Her face is the most striking aspect of this work. She looks angry and determined and her expression seems to warn anyone who might try to threaten her and her children. She is saying, "Back off, or deal with me!" As a mother myself, I was instantly drawn to this work and recognized that look on her face as the natural and universal instinct of mothers everywhere to protect their offspring.

Mary Beth Kass
Co-President
Bedford 2020 Coalition

The *Inuit Mother with Twins* reflects a very important theme in Inuit art—that of mother and child, which is often seen in prints as well as sculpture. This mother has two children that appear to be about one year old. One is in the "amautuk," which is a mother's coat with a very large hood that covers the child carried on her back. The other child is being fed from the mother's hand.

The carving is a relatively early work as far as Inuit sculpture goes. It was probably sculpted in the 1960's from a round piece of grey stone known as a "tent stone," a rock used at that time to hold down the bear-skin tents in which the people lived. It is striking how this everyday kind of material has been worked to create the feeling of tenderness of the mother for her children.

Elaine Blechman
Arctic Artistry Gallery

Ary Scheffer (1795-1858)
Portrait of René, Cécile, and Louise Franchomme, ca. 1850-51
Oil on canvas
29.75 x 25.625 inches
Richard L. Feigen & Company

Inspiring the voice within

Children give voice to the innocence and soul of music. Creativity takes flight, new worlds unfold and rigid traditions melt. Self becomes an expanded expression.

Take courage, inspire, and listen!

Jeffrey P. Haydon
Chief Executive Officer
Caramoor

Siblings carve up the world among themselves. Here the eldest daughter assumes a natural air of authority as the middle child proudly shows off his classical good looks, the instrument he holds in hand a kind of grace note underscoring his sublime self-assurance. What, though, of the latecomer? The wee girl peering intently from a corner of Scheffer's portrait looks to be old beyond her years. Hers are the thoughts we wonder about. She is the one we might wish to know. Scheffer painted this meditation on family affinity within a year of the publication of American Romantic Nathaniel Hawthorne's *Scarlet Letter*. Like Pearl, that story's beguiling young character, the little sister is an enigmatic presence. She is a spirit child whose first allegiance is not to family, but rather to some wellspring of inner wisdom that her older siblings, in all their worldliness and sophistication, have lost contact with forever.

Leonard S. Marcus
Historian, Critic, and Curator

Michael Ferris Jr. (b. 1969)
Toufic, 2010
Recycled wood, acrylic pigment
76 x 47 x 23 inches
Courtesy of the artist

***T**oufic* is a wonderfully eclectic piece that highlights the intricacies and complexities of the influences that comprise an individual. We are the sum of all of our experiences and generations of mixed ethnicities and cultures. Individually complex, but singularly beautiful.

So, too, is our community. As an elected official, I appreciate the vast diversity of Westchester County, a quarter of whose population is foreign-born. Out of the unique qualities of each individual and community, we weave a tapestry of strength, caring, and beauty.

Peter B. Harckham
Westchester County Board of Legislators
Legislator, 2nd District
Majority Leader

My first impression is of the bold decorative patterns. The patterns are at odds with the features of the face. The person appears to be an elderly Caucasian with a sad or tired gaze; he reminds me of a Florida retiree. The patterns remind me of Southeast Asia, perhaps Malaysia, Indonesia, or the Philippines. This causes me to speculate and develop a story for this person. Perhaps he lost his job or pension assets during the process of exporting jobs and is now suffering financially as a result of globalization.

The selection of wood, an organic material, makes the piece more emotionally accessible than if it were created with metal or stone. The face becomes more alive and animated. Then I think about the name of the piece, *Toufic*, and I think that this is an odd name if it is supposed to be the subject's name.

David Schunter
Principal
Andron Construction

Lucas Cranach (1472-1553)
*Sybilla: Daughter of the Elector Frederick
the Wise of Saxony as Mary Magdalen*
ca. 1530
Oil on panel
22.25 x 16.25 inches
Caramoor Rosen House Collection
Photo: Margaret Fox

The German painter and printmaker Lucas Cranach (1472-1553) worked in Vienna for a few years before 1505, when he went to Wittenberg to serve as court artist to Duke Frederick the Wise. He painted religious pictures, mythological scenes, and portraits, in all of which the female figures conform to a courtly ideal, one blending current taste with Cranach's own preferences. As in the panel from Caramoor, the women are slim and angular, with long necks and high brows, not unlike modern runway models. The comparison may be extended to facial expressions, which convey little more than vacuous contentment with one's appearance, expensive clothes, and presumed superiority to the viewer.

By contrast, Cranach's male portraits, including those of his friend Martin Luther and Henry the Pious, Duke of Saxony, convey individual character incisively. In their costumes, however, the artist's princely patrons seem as stiff as mannequins despite swords or other objects implying an active life (like polo mallets in the windows at Ralph Lauren). Of course, this frozen sense of form suits court portraiture, which functioned as icons of rulership. Objects that in the world of fashion would be called accessories, such as the looping gold chain worn as a necklace in this portrait, were intended by Cranach and his clients as attributes, or signifiers of rank.

In the Caramoor picture, the young lady holds an ointment jar suggesting that she, like Mary Magdalen in her later years, was a model of feminine virtue. The Magdalen is said to have anointed Christ on several occasions. Sybilla of Saxony is not known to have purveyed bath oils or been otherwise employed in her youth. But she would have approved an old saying about the Magdalen (variously attributed to John the Baptist, Truman Capote, and Mel Brooks): "It's not what you know, but who you know."

**Walter Liedtke
Curator of European Paintings
The Metropolitan Museum
of Art**

Sybilla
princess
prize
possession
Queen.

What word do they have
for a woman who loses ALL
of her children?

Did you love that Guy?
Your heart
a trinket traded
for title, for land
remains a secret.

Your face unfolds no fealty.

**Joanne Hudson
Actress**

Daniel Rozin (b. 1961)
Mirror No. 12, 2013
Video camera, custom software,
computer, projector, custom projection
on wood oval
34 x 60 inches
Courtesy of the artist and
bitforms gallery, NYC

Daniel Rozin's egg-shaped mirror hatches images of you in motion. When you move in front of it, you are transformed into a fluid series of rotating lines—fading in and out, dissolving, breaking apart, and blending into each other.

By interacting with *Mirror No. 12,* the artist enables you to become a polymorphic self-generated movie. Instead of reflecting you, this mirror invites you to reflect: Are you the movie you are watching? Or are you the person you watch watching the movie?

Frank Cantor
Filmmaker

This mirror seems to have created a world apart from us, and with it questions about how we experience reflections of ourselves.

Angles of incidence and reflection are broken. Time is sliced and stretched. Caught in its rift we watch Duchamp's nude descend the staircase. We submit to the pace of its movement, fascinated like a child with a bubble wand.

Daniel Rozin reminds us that we can't view art without collaborating with it. Our interaction is as much a part of the result as is his execution. After all, it's not always easy to tell who is contributing more—the author or the actor.

(Although seriously, Rozin has contributed the genius and effort here. You're pretty much just moving your arms around.)

Chris Wedge
Film Director

I find Jason Salavon's portrait of Rembrandt both ancient and extremely contemporary. It takes courage to produce a portrait of one of history's most important portrait artists. Staring at Salavon's Rembrandt it is somewhat difficult to actually locate Rembrandt. He seems always to be in motion, moving in front of us, somewhat blurred. This is because Salavon has overlaid all of Rembrandt's self-portraits onto each other. We are seeing glimpses of an elusive Rembrandt at the same time that we are seeing his whole life. He is present and mysterious. We might conclude that old masters never die and they don't fade away. Salavon knowingly makes us aware that great art can live again, even in a timeframe never imagined by the artist who created it. This is also a portrait of Salavon, an explorer of new technology. It is a handshake from one generation to another.

Ronald Feldman
Ronald Feldman Fine Arts, Inc.

The good painter, like the good poet, pays close attention to detail and we benefit from this artistic scrutiny. It allows us the opportunity to "see" in a way we haven't before.

With this in mind, I find much dramatic irony and some religiosity in Jason Salavon's portrait of Rembrandt. Salavon has taken Rembrandt's own self-portraits and obliterated his identifying visage—though not entirely. In the shadow of eyes, nose, mouth, and chin, we have what appears to be a saintly glow, a halo.

Is it possible that Salavon, with enormous admiration for his subject, is stealing Rembrandt's identity in order to find what is missing in himself? While manipulating data on the computer, he reveals what is essential and enduring while discarding the rest. Or as Fellini said, "The pearl is the oyster's autobiography."

With virtual paint, brush, and possibly Photoshop's spot healing tool (this is where the poetry comes in), one artist has reimagined another and we are transformed.

Myrna Goodman
Poet and Artist

Alexandre-Jean Dubois-Drahonet
(1791-1834)
Portrait of Guillaume-Gervais Millet
1816
Oil on canvas
21 x 17.5 inches
Richard L. Feigen & Company

Seven Veterans Assess a Soldier

He needs a haircut.
Immature child.
Too much bling.
Does not impress me.
Educated, inexperienced, and young.
Revolutionary war veteran from Spain.
Paul McCartney from *Sgt. Pepper's
    Lonely Hearts Club Band*.

**Submitted by Veterans at the
American Legion
Katonah Post 1575**

Anticipating what is yet to come, after what has been, can unhinge a man. It can turn his stomach and slash his resolve. Think war. Add combat. Friction. Uncertainty. Noise, lots of it. Friendship. Brotherhood. And of course, death. Now take that man and immediately remove him from the battlefield. Bring him back home. Away from his buddies, the noise, the adrenaline. Sit him with his family around a dinner table. Where they ask too many questions. Then dress him up and paint his portrait. All the while, the clock is ticking. And he knows it. Enjoy the food. Love your family. Drink heavily. But, he is going back to War. Soon. Guillaume-Gervais Millet is going back.

This portrait is a perfect snapshot of Mr. Millet in the eye of the storm, where the past and the future meet simultaneously. Knowing and fearing. Utter dread. Where duty and loyalty are the only things that keep him going. Let me leave you with these stanzas from a poem by Siegfried Sassoon, which capture this sentiment exactly. Haunted by the past, he fears the future and is caught because of his loyalty to those he left behind.

*When I'm asleep, dreaming and drowsed and warm,
They come, the homeless ones, the noiseless dead.
While the dim charging breakers of the storm
Rumble and drone and bellow overhead,*

*Out of the gloom they gather about my bed.
They whisper to my heart; their thoughts are mine.*

*...And while the dawn begins with slashing rain
I think of the Battalion in the mud.
'When are you going back to them again?
'Are they not still your brothers through our blood?'*

**1LT William S. Rago
4-31 IN, 2 BCT, 10TH MTN DIV (LI)**

Did You Know?
Curatorial information

American School
Mary Elizabeth Knickerbacker, 19th century
Oil on canvas
27 x 23 inches
Private collection of William Kelly Simpson

American School
Joseph Foster Knickerbacker, 19th century
Oil on canvas
27 x 23 inches
Private collection of William Kelly Simpson

Joseph Foster (1824-1882) and Mary Elizabeth (1830-1846) Knickerbacker were half-siblings, the children of Abraham Knickerbacker. Although she appears older, Miss Knickerbacker was 16 at the time this portrait was painted. She tragically died one week before her high school graduation from the Troy Seminary School. Her half-brother Joseph was born with a birth defect that stunted the growth of his arms and he remained a recluse much of his life. He was a poet; his most notable work was *A Vision of the Arch of Truth*, published in 1876.

These two portraits have been passed down through multiple generations of Knickerbackers and remain in the family's possession today. The surname Knickerbacker (later Knickerbocker) is synonymous with the 17th-century Dutch settlers of New York State, specifically in the Mohawk and Upper Hudson Valley regions. The family settled one of their earliest ancestral homes, Knickerbocker Mansion, in Schaghticoke, NY, around 1700, where these half siblings were born and spent their entire lives.

Diane Arbus (1923-1971)
Soothsayer Madame Sandra, California, 1963
Gelatin silver print, printed later by Selkirk
14.5 x 14.5 inches
Private collection
© The Estate of Diane Arbus

Look closely—Diane Arbus's inverted silhouette is reflected in Madame Sandra's crystal ball. Her ghostly presence in this otherwise banal scene seems appropriate for the artist, who has attained mythic status since her suicide. Her honest and dignified portrayals of people on the margins of society continue to resonate today.

Arbus took this photograph of Madame Sandra soon after she switched from a 35 mm camera to the twin-lens Rolleiflex that produced her trademark square prints. Neil Selkirk, a British photographer based in New York City, is the only person authorized by the Arbus estate to print her photographs, a responsibility he has had for over 40 years.

Robert Arneson (1930-1992)
I Have My Eyes on Me Endlessly, 1992
Bronze
80 x 12 x 12 inches
Courtesy of George Adams Gallery, New York
© Estate of Robert Arneson / Licensed by VAGA, New York, NY

Robert Arneson cast this bronze self-portrait in 1992—the same year as his death from cancer. Initially humorous, the totem-like sculpture also conveys the deep inner reflection of a man facing mortality. Arneson is best remembered for his highly influential and irreverent ceramic portraits, although he worked extensively in bronze the final years of his life.

Cecil Beaton (1904-1980)
Portrait of Lucie B. Rosen, ca. 1932
Pencil, watercolor, and gouache on paper
16.5 x 11.5 inches
Caramoor Rosen House Collection

A fashion and society photographer for *Vanity Fair* and *Vogue* in the 1920s, Sir Cecil Beaton painted this elegant and stylized portrait of Lucie Bigelow Rosen posed in her townhouse on West 54th Street (Beaton cunningly includes his own image reflected in the gold framed mirror). Lucie and her husband Walter owned Caramoor, an estate in Katonah they used as a summer residence from 1928 until 1945, after which they bequeathed it to the public as a center for music and the arts. The 18th-century crystal candelabras, the Chinese turquoise brush holder on the fireplace mantle, and the small bronze cassolette (container) on the side table in Beaton's painting are on display in the Rosen House at Caramoor today.

Jonathan Becker (b. 1954)
Saturday Night Live in Elaine's Kitchen, 1975
Archival pigment print
24 x 24 inches
Courtesy of Jonathan Becker/
Steven Kasher Gallery, NY
© Jonathan Becker

Undoubtedly taken in the early morning hours, Jonathan Becker shot this photograph in 1975, the first season of *Saturday Night Live*. He captures original cast members Chevy Chase, Dan Aykroyd, and John Belushi as well as producer Lorne Michaels.

Mentored by legendary photographer Brassaï, Becker has been a contributing photographer to *Vanity Fair* since 1990. He has portrayed luminaries from the worlds of art, literature, and politics, as well as pop culture and high society.

Louis-Léopold Boilly (1761-1845)
Grimacing Man (Self-Portrait), ca. 1822-23
Black chalk with touches of white and red chalk on light brown (formerly blue) wove paper
9.75 x 7.75 inches
Private collection

French artist Louis-Léopold Boilly was a young prodigy who painted as many as 5,000 portraits, most of them flattering images of his fashionable middle-class clientele. He was a gifted visual storyteller and an astute observer of bourgeois urban life during the Napoleonic era. His mischievous side surfaced not only in his genre scenes, but also in his witty paintings, drawings, and lithographs of "grimaces," to which this self-portrait belongs. Boilly's masterful print, *Thirty-six Faces of Expression* (1825), illustrates the scope of the artist's investigation into changing emotional states.

Chinese
Ancestor Portrait, ca. 1860
Ink and mineral colors on tightly woven silk, mounted on paper
57.5 x 37.5 inches
Lisbeth and Frank Stern

Chinese families commissioned ancestor portraits as expressions of filial devotion and objects of veneration. Traditionally, incense was burned on a low table in front of the portrait where food, wine, and flowers were offered in the belief that the spirit of the ancestor could bring good luck, long life, wealth, and male offspring.

Artists, mostly anonymous, took great care in painting an ancestor's face, using sample books, verbal descriptions, and the observation of familial similarities to create an authentic likeness of the dearly departed. This ancestor is typical in that he looks straight out and engages the viewer, although he appears more benevolent and less severe than most. Except for his face, the painting style is flat and was typically finished by lesser artisans using stencils.

From his clothing and accoutrements, we can surmise that this gentleman was a civil official. The ruby knob on his hat and the patch on his blue velvet coat, depicting a silver pheasant or paradise flycatcher, define his rank. The elegantly patterned Oriental rug proclaims his wealth while long finger nails indicate his exemption from manual labor.

Chuck Close (b. 1940)
Emma, 2002
113-color hand printed ukiyo-e woodcut, edition of 55
36 x 30 inches
Private collection
© Chuck Close, courtesy Pace Gallery

Chuck Close paints only the faces of people he knows; this is a portrait of his niece, Emma. Close collaborated with master printer Yasu Shibata to create this print based on an original painting. It was executed in the 17th-century Japanese technique of relief printing known as ukiyo-e. Shibata hand carved each of the 27 large wooden printing blocks and used 113 colors. While Close's painting of Emma took three months to complete, the printmaking process took a year and a half. Says Shibata, "I think *Emma* is the biggest Japanese-style woodblock ever made." http://chuckclose.coe.uh.edu/process/emma.htm

John Singleton Copley (1738-1815)
Mrs. John Scollay (Mercy Greenleaf), 1763
Oil on canvas
35.25 x 28 inches
Driscoll Babcock

Arguably the greatest portraitist in colonial America, John Singleton Copley produced this country's most elegant and finely crafted paintings of the 18th century. He portrayed patriots such as Paul Revere and John Hancock, as well as prosperous members of New England's rising merchant class. Copley's innate artistic talent and genial personality led to huge social and financial success. His solid modeling and ability to faithfully render flesh, hair, textiles, and reflections were unlike anything seen before in the colonies.
http://www.worcesterart.org/Collection/Early_American/Artists/copley/biography/

Gustave Courbet (1819-1877)
Portrait of Jo, 1865
Oil on paper, mounted on mahogany board
10.625 x 8.5 inches
Private collection

The Irish model Joanna ("Jo") Hiffernan posed for several of Gustave Courbet's most famous paintings, including *La Belle Irlandaise* at the Metropolitan Museum of Art and the erotic *L'Origine du Monde* at the Musée d'Orsay. Courbet, a pioneer and leader of the Realist movement, met Hiffernan through his acquaintance with American artist James McNeill Whistler when both summered in Trouville on the Normandy coast in 1865. (Hiffernan was Whistler's mistress for six years; his *Symphony in White, No. I: The White Girl* is of Jo.) In 1865, when this image was painted, Courbet wrote of "the beauty of a superb redhead whose portrait I have begun."
http://www.metmuseum.org/toah/works-of-art/29.100.63

Lucas Cranach (1472-1553)
Sybilla: Daughter of the Elector Frederick the Wise of Saxony as Mary Magdalen, ca. 1530
Oil on panel
22.25 x 16.25 inches
Caramoor Rosen House Collection

In 1505, Duke Friedrich III (Friedrich the Wise), Elector of Saxony, appointed Lucas Cranach his court painter. Cranach served Friedrich and his successors for the remainder of his life, becoming a celebrated artist and a wealthy man.

Cranach is the artist most closely affiliated with the Protestant Reformation. He made portraits of his close friend Martin Luther and other leaders of the movement. Cranach embraced Luther's teachings and, in addition to his courtly duties, developed a new repertoire of religious subjects, or adapted traditional ones, to reflect Protestant ideals. Today, more than 1,500 paintings by Cranach and his prolific Wittenberg workshop are known, although they represent only a small fraction of the works originally produced.
http://www.metmuseum.org/toah/hd/refo/hd_refo.htm
http://www.lucascranach.org/aboutus_en.html

Edward Curtis (1868-1952)
Nalin, Apache Portrait, 1903
Photogravure
17 x 13 inches
Collection of Steven and Nevine Michaan

Edward Curtis is the best known photographer of the American West and its native peoples. In 1906, at President Theodore Roosevelt's recommendation, J. P. Morgan helped finance Curtis's efforts to produce the monumental, 20-volume publication *The North American Indian*. During this 20-year project, Curtis visited 80 different tribes west of the Mississippi River and took over 40,000 images. He recorded rituals, costumes, tribal dances, tribal lore, history, and biographical sketches.

Prior to embarking on the project, Curtis made this photogravure of the young Apache girl Nalin, who was possibly a member of the Warm Springs Chiricahua Apache tribe of New Mexico. Curtis captures her in a strict frontal pose with a neutral studio backdrop.
http://nmai.si.edu/searchcollections/item.aspx?irn=321279

Matteo de' Pasti
Isotta degli Atti of Rimini (born 1432/33, died 1474)
12
Bronze alloy, cast
Diameter 85.20 mm (3.35 inches)
Courtesy of Frances Beatty and Allen Adler

The secular and clerical elite of the Italian Renaissance were as conscious of their place in history as they were anxious to demonstrate and consolidate their temporal power. Taking ancient Roman coins as a model, they developed the idea of the medal. Unlike coins, having no intrinsic value, these small discs were cast to commemorate important social and political events as well as personal milestones. They provided a durable and long-lasting record of the sitter's physical attributes, as well as their achievements. Occasionally they were used to adorn clothing or worn as a pendant, but they were mostly enjoyed as intimate hand-held sculptures and as objects of aesthetic and intellectual contemplation.

Artist Matteo de' Pasti portrays the teenage beauty Isotta degli Atti on this medal commissioned by her husband Sigismondo Malatesta, the Duke of Rimini. Although cast later, probably in 1449, the medal bears the date of 1446, the year Sigismondo won the 13-year-old as his mistress (Isotta and Sigismondo married in 1456). Cast at the height of Sigismondo's political power, the medal was intended to secure and enhance Isotta's reputation for posterity. Roses and the elephant seen on the reverse were heraldic devices of the Malatesta family, symbolizing strength, fame, and immortality, as well as the virtues of piety and chastity. Sigismondo had dozens of these medals embedded in the walls and foundations of his buildings for future generations to discover.

Alexandre-Jean Dubois-Drahonet
(1791-1834)
Portrait of Guillaume-Gervais Millet, 1816
Oil on canvas
21 x 17.5 inches
Richard L. Feigen & Company

Guillaume-Gervais Millet was a surgeon major of the mounted officers of the French Royal Guard. He proudly wears the medal of the Legion of Honor, the highest decoration awarded in France. The details of the young surgeon's costume are painted with great care, reflecting the artist's fascination with military dress. Alexandre-Jean Dubois-Drahonet was a distinguished neoclassical painter of portraits and military costumes. In 1832, King William IV of England commissioned Dubois-Drahonet to paint 100 miniatures of uniformed officers of the British Army and Navy (now housed in the Royal Collection at Windsor Castle).

Eastern Tibet
Champa Kunga Tendzin, an abbot of Ngor, 1862-70
Distemper on cloth
72 x 44 inches
Private collection

Tibetan thangkas (also referred to as tangka, thanka, or tanka, meaning "recorded message") are paintings on cotton or silk that serve as vehicles for devotion and meditation. Originating in Nepal, the custom reached Tibet in the 9th or 10th century, when its form had already evolved into a fabric scroll that could be easily transported by a lama teaching Buddhist philosophy.

Thangka artists, mostly anonymous, acquired their skills through long religious devotion and apprenticeship. Every element has a meaning, including the colors, gestures, poses, and objects, while strict guidelines define the measurements and proportions for each deity. The subjects are mainly Buddhas and bodhisativas (enlightened beings), lamas (teachers who have reached a level of spiritual attainment), mandalas (circle designs representing the universe and used for meditation), traditional medicine, and historical events.

This thangka portrays Champa Kunga Tendzin, a 19th-century abbot of Ngor. A once-thriving Buddhist monastery founded in 1429 in central Tibet, Ngor was largely destroyed by the Chinese in 1959.

Egyptian
Head of Amenhotep III, New Kingdom Dynasty XVIII, ca. 1390-1380 BC
Green basalt
6.25 x 4 x 4 inches
Private collection of William Kelly Simpson

The New Kingdom of ancient Egypt, or the period between the 16th century and 11th century BC, was Egypt's most prosperous time and marked the peak of its power. Amenhotep III ruled for nearly 40 years during the 18th Dynasty of Egypt's history. Under his rule as pharaoh, Egypt experienced an impressive period of artistic creativity. His own mortuary temple was known to be the largest single temple in Egypt, although only two statues remain at its ruins today. He was also responsible for the building of the temple of Luxor. As the arts flourished under his reign, portraiture in ancient Egypt became highly developed. The belief in life after death, and the emphasis on preserving the past, attributed to the extensive surge in portrait sculpture during this period.

Michael Ferris Jr. (b. 1969)
Toufic, 2010
Recycled wood, acrylic pigment
76 x 47 x 23 inches
Courtesy of the artist

Michael Ferris constructs his portraits from reclaimed wood and pigmented grout. He builds, grinds, chisels, and sands his forms before adding the ornamental surfaces. According to the artist, his laborious process "becomes very interesting to me near the end as I work to find the correct balance between the form, the patterned surface, and the presence of the person I am sculpting."

The monumental *Toufic* is a portrait of the artist's uncle who lives in Lebanon. Ferris credits two finely inlaid Syrian backgammon boards from his childhood home as inspiration for his intricate mosaic craftsmanship ("They amazed me"). The dense abstract designs pay homage to Ferris's father, a Lebanese Maronite, and to his Middle Eastern heritage.

Howard Finster (1916-2001)
Little Punch, 1984
Paint on wood
56 x 24 inches
Private collection

Little Punch was Howard Finster's 3,572nd artwork. Educated only through the sixth grade, Finster became a Baptist preacher who, at age 60, had a vision to spread the gospel through painting religious art, something he had never done before. Finster vowed to paint 5,000 pictures; he reached his goal in 1985, but kept on going. At the time of his death in 2001, Finster's works numbered over 46,000 and included both sacred and secular subjects. He remains one of America's most acclaimed Outsider artists.

Eric Fischl (b. 1948)
The Krakoffs, 2006
Oil on linen
78.25 x 58.5 inches
© Eric Fischl, Courtesy Mary Boone Gallery, New York

Eric Fischl's portrait depicts New York power couple Delphine and Reed Krakoff. She is a home designer and he is president and executive creative director at Coach as well as the eponymous Reed Krakoff Collection, launched in 2010. They are also passionate art collectors.

Fischl is noted for his enigmatic and provocative paintings of people who often appear unaware of the artist's perceptive gaze. He captures moments that are private and perhaps secret, turning viewers into voyeurs.

Martine Franck (1938-2012)
Portrait of Henri Cartier-Bresson, 1992
Modern gelatin silver print
16 x 20 inches
Collection of Ellen and Robert Grimes
Courtesy Magnum Photos

Martine Franck took this ingenious triple-portrait of her husband in 1992. Both photographers were reticent about having their pictures taken and neither was a willing subject for the other. Franck was a busy freelance photographer in Paris in 1966, on assignment for magazines like *Vogue*, *Life*, and *Sports Illustrated* when she met her future husband. Thirty years her senior, Henri Cartier-Bresson was already internationally renowned as the father of photojournalism. "His opening line was, 'Martine, I want to come and see your contact sheets,' " she said of Cartier-Bresson in a 2010 television interview with Charlie Rose. They were married in 1970.
http://www.nytimes.com/2012/08/23/arts/martine-franck-documentary-photographer-dies-at-74.html?_r=0

Christopher French (b. 1957)
Vital Statistics CY, 1998
Oil on chromogenic photographic paper mounted on wood panel
24 x 18 inches
Courtesy of the artist

Christopher French explores identity and how it is presented to the world. In *Vital Statistics CY*, he simultaneously depicts three classifications of identity, combining outward appearances with innate characteristics. The "CY" in his title refers to Catherine Yelloz, the artist's friend and subject. French partially masks her face with a painted fingerprint, which was enlarged from her index finger. The raised Braille letters list seven of Yelloz's identifying characteristics—the same information found on a driver's license or a police record. From top to bottom, the statistics are: date of birth, Social Security number, race, height, weight, hair color, and eye color.

Anne-Karin Furunes (b. 1961)
Portraits of Archive Pictures, VIII, 2011
Acrylic painted canvas, perforated
88.25 x 63 inches
Courtesy of Barry Friedman Ltd.

Anne-Karin Furunes has developed a unique process of representation that involves punching circular holes in 30 different sizes through canvas. Her paintings require viewers to move around to find the right focal distance at which the eye blends the "dots" into smooth tones to resolve the image, similar to halftone reproductions. Paradoxically, it is through the negative, pixelated spaces that Furunes reveals her subjects. She suggests that, like memories or history, her images are clear from a distance but disappear as viewers come closer and try to grasp them. "I always come back to the portrait," she says, "because the portrait tells so much about how it is to be human."

Felix Gonzalez-Torres (1957-1996)
"Untitled" (Portrait of Dad), 1991
White candies individually wrapped in cellophane, endless supply
Overall dimensions vary with installation
Ideal weight 175 lbs
© The Felix Gonzalez-Torres Foundation
Courtesy of Andrea Rosen Gallery, New York

Untitled (Portrait of Dad) is Felix Gonzalez-Torres's allegorical representation of his father. The aggregate weight of the white mint candies is the same as his father's—175 pounds. Visitors are invited to take pieces of candy; as the pile diminishes, the candy is restocked. It is an eternal cycle of loss and renewal. Gonzalez-Torres's art invites viewer participation: "I need the viewer, I need the public interaction. Without a public these works are nothing, nothing. I need the public to complete the work. I ask the public to help me, to take responsibility, to become part of my work, to join in."

Ken Grimes (b. 1947)
Untitled (Alien entities), 2006
Acrylic on panel
48 x 72 inches
Private collection

A few years after Ken Grimes experienced his first psychotic break, the self-taught artist began recording his ideas about extraterrestrials and the paranormal on canvas. He starts his compositions by sketching in pencil and then using black acrylic paint to outline the figures and letters, leaving sections of the white canvas exposed. Grimes claims this arduous technique results in more sharply defined images than could be achieved by simply painting white over a black background.

Untitled (Alien entities) depicts a dozen portraits of extraterrestrials that the artist has seen here on earth. Each is unique, yet they exhibit features commonly associated with aliens in comic books and science fiction films.

Red Grooms (b. 1937)
Mondrian, 1990
Painted bronze
24 x 19 x 14.75 inches
Louis-Dreyfus Family Collection
©2013 Red Grooms/Artists Rights Society (ARS), New York

Red Grooms's sculptural portrait of Piet Mondrian (1872-1944) is part of a larger body of work portraying famous artists. Grooms's whimsical idea to enclose Mondrian in his signature grid is revealing and humorous. Mondrian was serious, philosophical, and almost as austere as his reductive, geometric paintings. Dressed in a suit and tie with glasses and a pipe, he resembles a college professor more than the stereotypical bohemian artist. Grooms incorporates symbols of Mondrian's art, such as an ink bottle and the primary colors, into the composition. Elements from the artist's personal life are also displayed on the gridded structure (although the comb is a mystery for a man with no hair!).

Duane Hanson (1925-1996)
Charlie, 1990
Bronze, polychromed with oil, mixed media with accessories
71 x 30 x 23 inches
Collection of Sondra Peterson
© Estate of Duane Hanson / Licensed by VAGA, New York, NY

Duane Hanson's sculptures are so realistic that museum visitors often mistake them for real people. Many of his lifelike figures are made of flesh-colored polyester resin, but *Charlie* is cast in bronze and painted. Hanson attends to every minute detail, from hangnails to razor stubble. A wig, glasses, hat, and clothing complete the illusion. Of his art Hanson said, "I'm mostly interested in the human form as subject matter and means of expression for my sculpture. What can generate more

interest, fascination, beauty, ugliness, joy, shock, or contempt than a human being?" Posed as a security guard, *Charlie* appears bored on the job.
http://learn.michenerartmuseum.org/wp-content/uploads/2009/08/curriculum-duane-hanson.pdf

Joseph Hardin (1921-1989)
Marilyn Monroe, 1989
Paint on poster board
10 x 14 inches
Collection of Audrey B. Heckler

Wheelchair-bound from rheumatoid arthritis since age seven, Joseph Hardin's mobility was restricted to only his shoulders and arm joints; his crippled hands could hardly maneuver a paintbrush. Virginia Martin, a fellow Birmingham, Alabama resident, discovered Hardin's artistic talent when she arrived at his government-subsidized apartment to deliver "Meals on Wheels." Moved by his determination to create art, she brought him cardboard and painting supplies in addition to his lunches and dinners. Martin also took his finished paintings to art fairs and potential collectors. It is due to her dedication that Hardin gained recognition for his intensely personal and visionary art.
http://www.marciaweberartobjects.com/hardin.html

Robert Henri (1865-1929)
Portrait of Marcia Ann M. Tucker, 1926
Oil on canvas
60 x 40.5 inches
Driscoll Babcock

Marcia Anne M. Tucker (1915-1955) was the daughter of Carll and Marcia Tucker of Park Avenue and Bedford, New York. They were owners of Penwood, one of the grandest estates in Westchester County. The property sat on three hundred acres enclosed by what is today South Bedford Road to Guard Hill Road, and West Patent Road to McClain Street.

Artist Robert Henri appropriately poses 11-year-old Marcia on a Louis XV fauteuil chair and presents her youthful beauty against a dark, neutral background. Henri died three years after painting this portrait, and the sitter herself was dead by age 40. A decade later the construction of Interstate 684 divided the Penwood estate; the property was ultimately sold and subdivided into "newer mansions" in the 1990s.

Oliver Herring (b. 1964)
Gloria, 2004
Digital C-print photographs, museum board, foam core, and polystyrene
72 x 40 x 40 inches
Courtesy of the artist and Max Protetch

Oliver Herring's *Gloria* is a remarkable life-size portrait collage. The artist first photographed his model from every conceivable angle, then adhered thousands of sliced pictures to a full-size Styrofoam form. Herring doesn't miss a thing, from *Gloria*'s chipped nail polish to the incredible treatment of her hair. He successfully creates a feeling of ennui; the barefoot *Gloria* idly plays with her necklace while seemingly lost in thought. Through his ingenious manipulation, viewers can sense the "weight" of the woman leaning against the Plexiglas frame.

Igbo (Ibo) tribe, Nigeria
Maiden Spirit Mask, 1903
Painted wood
18 inches high
Arctic Artistry Gallery

This *Maiden Spirit Mask* would have been worn during a celebration marking a girl's coming of age in the Igbo tribe of Southeastern Nigeria. The ceremony, featuring music and dance performed before multiple spectators, pays homage to feminine beauty.

Although traditionally worn by a young man, the mask depicts an adolescent girl in exaggerated perfection. The elongated face, straight nose, and smooth pale skin are considered attributes of good character, grace, and dignity. The light face, achieved with white chalk or kaolin, indicates that a spiritual quality has been achieved, while the dark scarification features reflect Igbo aesthetics. The complex hairstyle is elaborately carved and colored. At a foot and a half in height, the mask concealed its wearer's identity. Undoubtedly heavy, it would have been cumbersome and hot for the performer of the ceremonial dance.

Indian, Master of the School of Mankot
Portrait of Raja Mahipat Dev, ca. 1690-1710
7.5 x 11 inches
Opaque watercolor on paper
David Swope

Art flourished in the kingdom of Mankot, located in the mountainous region of Northern India, from the 17th to the

19th century, particularly in the form of miniatures. This painting portrays Raja Mahipat Dev of Mankot seated in prayer. The Raja was a devout Hindu follower of the Vaishnavite sect. The white marking on his forehead, called tilak, is a public sign of his spiritual devotion to Vishnu (Raja Mahipat Dev was the first Mankot ruler to be portrayed with tilak marks). It is perhaps a winter setting as he is fully covered in a double cloth. This painting is among the few portraits of Raja Mahipat Dev in existence today.

Byron Kim (b. 1961)
Emmett at Twelve Months, 1994
Egg tempera on panel, Suite of 25 paintings
3 x 2.5 x .75 inches each
17 x 14.5 x .75 inches
Courtesy of the artist and James Cohan Gallery, New York / Shanghai

Byron Kim challenges traditional classifications of race and ethnicity. Kim gained international recognition at the 1993 Whitney Biennial with his minimalist painting replicating people's skin tones. The title of the work, *Synecdoche*, is a figure of speech in which a part of something is used to describe the whole, or vice-versa. *Emmett at Twelve Months* is part of this continued exploration. Here Kim faithfully replicates all the colors found on his young son's body. Kim called *Synecdoche* "a strange project because I am making abstract paintings but their subject matter is so concrete. In a sense these paintings are repesentational, even figurative."
Donna De Salvo, *Face Value: American Portraits* (Southampton, New York: The Parrish Art Museum, 1995), p. 28.

Käthe Kollwitz (1867-1945)
Self-Portrait, 1921
Etching on cream Japan paper, signed lower right
8.75 x 10.5 inches
Courtesy Galerie St. Etienne, New York

The tragedies of war, poverty, and social injustice were common themes in Käthe Kollwitz's art. Her life and work were forever shaped by the tragic loss of her son Peter in combat in 1914. Her direct experience with war is still evident in this self-portrait etching seven years later. As Kollwitz's heavy head rests on her large, almost oversized hand, the emotional and physical weight is palpable. She glances away from the viewer, but her deep sadness is both

obvious and jarring. The clash of vertical and horizontal lines adds poignancy to the rendering.

Mende, Sierra Leone
Dance Mask, Early 20th century
Carved wood
14.5 inches high
Bruce Frank Primitive Art

Unique in Sub-Saharan countries, a woman, not a man, would have exclusively worn this dance mask. Senior members of the Sande women's secret society don these masks, along with blackened raffia collars and robes, to perform ritualistic dances at initiation ceremonies, funerals, and important tribal events. This mask, with a smooth and highly polished surface, fits over the head like a helmet. With its elaborate carved hairstyle, delicate facial features, high forehead, and horizontal lines at the neck representing voluptuous rolls of skin, the mask captures Sande ideals of feminine beauty. Today it is estimated that the Sande society has 1.5 million members.

This mask comes from the Mende tribe, one of the largest ethnic groups in Sierra Leone, West Africa. A Sande official likely commissioned a male artisan to carve it from a hollowed tree trunk. Its glossy sheen comes from decades of use and palm oil applications. The mask was previously in the collection of William Siegmann, a leading expert on the art and masquerades of Liberia and Sierra Leone.

Moche
Portrait Head of Cut Lip with Large Facial Stripes, ca. 100-800 AD
Terracotta
7.5 x inches high
Courtesy of Samuel Merrin
The Merrin Gallery

Moche
Portrait Head Fragment, ca. 400-550 AD
Terracotta
6.75 x inches high
Courtesy of Samuel Merrin
The Merrin Gallery

Their identities long forgotten, these two terracotta vessels represent distinct individuals within Moche society, a pre-Columbian civilization that flourished from about 100 to 800 AD in what is today northern Peru. This advanced and thriving culture had intricate irrigation systems, monumental architecture, elegant textile arts, and

some of the most varied pottery in the world. The majority of vessels—ranging from naturalistic to fantastic, from functional to ceremonial—are typically slip painted with red decoration on a cream background. Due to the high volume found in tombs, the vessels were originally thought to serve as funerary offerings; recent excavations in residential areas suggest that a great variety were also produced for everyday domestic Moche life.
http://www.metmuseum.org/toah/hd/moch/hd_moch.htm

Yasumasa Morimura (b. 1951)
Mona Lisa in Its Origins, 1998
Color photograph on canvas
30.5 x 21.5 inches
Private collection
Courtesy of the artist and
Luhring Augustine, New York

In this rather unsettling deconstruction of one of the most iconic images in the history of art, Yasumasa Morimura satirizes and simultaneously pays homage to Leonardo da Vinci's *Mona Lisa*. Morimura stars as his own model—a Japanese man transformed into an Italian woman with the world-famous smile. He uses painted backdrops, historic costumes, props, make-up, and digital manipulation to create his images. Morimura has appropriated portraits by such renowned artists as Van Gogh, Michelangelo, Velasquez, and Vermeer.

Vik Muniz (b. 1961)
Marilyn Monroe (from *Pictures of Diamonds*), 2004
Cibachrome print
40 x 30 inches
Collection of Ashley and Jim Diamond
© Vik Muniz / Licensed by VAGA,
New York, NY

Vik Muniz creates art with such unorthodox materials as sand, chocolate syrup, peanut butter, dust, and diamonds. This image of Marilyn Monroe is from his *Diamond Divas* series. Kwiat Jewelers loaned the artist more than 3,000 loose diamonds to define Monroe's famous face. Muniz cleverly references Pop artist Andy Warhol's 1960s screenprints of the Hollywood starlet. Interestingly, Warhol himself appropriated Monroe's image from a 1953 publicity still for the movie *Niagara*.
http://www.moma.org/learn/moma_learning/andy-warhol-gold-marilyn-monroe-1962

Alice Neel (1900-1984)
Portrait of Raphael Soyer, 1970
Oil on canvas
40 x 30 inches
Louis-Dreyfus Family Collection
© The Estate of Alice Neel
Courtesy David Zwirner, New York/London

Alice Neel was an early feminist and an artistic renegade who never followed the prevailing abstract styles. Portraits were her passion. Through her distinct linear approach and expressionistic use of color, Neel reveals her subjects' personalities, moods, even quirks. "Like Chekov, I am a collector of souls," she said. "I think if I hadn't been an artist I could have been a psychiatrist." Slouched in a chair and dressed in a rumpled suit, fellow artist Raphael Soyer (1899–1987) was a longtime friend of Neel's. She portrays the Social Realist painter with empathy, paying particular attention to his furrowed brow and knotty, veined hands.

Shirin Neshat (b. 1957)
I Am Its Secret, 1993
RC print and ink (photo taken by Plauto)
18.875 x 12.5 inches
Collection of Ashley and Jim Diamond
© Shirin Neshat
Courtesy of the artist and Gladstone Gallery, New York and Brussels

I Am Its Secret is part of Shirin Neshat's stark black-and-white photographic series entitled *Women of Allah*. Born and raised in Iran, Neshat's conceptual narratives confront issues of female identity in her native country. The artist posed for each image in the series; she hired a professional to take the shots. The swirling Farsi calligraphy, written directly on the photographic print, transcribes the poem, "I Will Greet the Sun Again," by Iranian feminist poet Forugh Farrokhzad. Neshat says, "I feel the use of poetry is particularly apt because literature has historically played a major part in the struggle against political repression. The poetry is the literal and symbolic voice of women whose sexuality and individualism have been obliterated by the chador or the veil."
http://quod.lib.umich.edu/cgi/t/text/text-idx?cc=mqr;c=mqr;c=mqrarchive;idno=act2080.0038.207;rgn=main;view=text;xc=1;g=mqrg

Julian Opie (b. 1958)
This is Monique, 2004
Continuous computer animation, computer film, PC, and 19 inch LCD screen,
Edition 4 of 4
Private collection
Courtesy of Barbara Krakow Gallery, Boston

At once generic and specific, Julian Opie's art is graphic, stylized, and fun. Monique, a Swiss art collector, commissioned the British artist to create this portrait of her. With seemingly childlike simplicity, Opie deftly defines *Monique*'s facial features with only eight black marks. Computer animation brings her to life, inviting viewer interaction and response. Opie's frank title serves as a formal introduction.

Makusi Panqutu (1933-1973)
Inuit Mother with Twins, ca. 1960
Grey stone
15 x 14 x 12 inches
Arctic Artistry Gallery

Inuit, a word meaning "people," denotes the aboriginal inhabitants of the North American Arctic (formerly known as Eskimos). Makusi Panqutu lived and worked in the community of Povungnituk (Puvirnituq), a settlement on the east coast of the Hudson Bay at the mouth of the Povungnituk River in Arctic Quebec. A Catholic mission was established there in 1956 and two years later, Father Andre Steinmann encouraged residents to form the Povungnituk Sculptors Society, allowing them to control their art sales and prices. Makusi Pangutu was one of the earliest sculptors from this region. Accessible only by air, Povungnituk has a current population of nearly 1,700 and remains a center of Inuit arts.

Gordon Parks (1912-2006)
Little Richard, Harlem, New York, 1967
Archival pigment print
14 x 11 inches
Courtesy The Gordon Parks Foundation
© The Gordon Parks Foundation

In the fall of 1967, Gordon Parks spent a month photographing the daily life of the Fontenelles, a desperately impoverished family in Harlem, New York. The following year, a photo essay was published in *Life* magazine containing 26 of the pictures in a special feature covering race and poverty in American cities. Parks said, "I wanted to show what it was like, the real, vivid horror of it—and the dignity of the people who

manage, somehow, to live with it." This photograph is of three-year-old Richard, the youngest of the Fontenelle's eight children. The caption that went with the image in the magazine read "[His mother] Bessie can't stop Little Richard from eating plaster. His lips stay cracked and swollen."

Pablo Picasso (1881-1973)
Tête d'homme barbu à la cigarette, 1964
Colored crayon on paper
25.75 x 19.75 inches
Private collection
©2013 Estate of Pablo Picasso/Artists Rights Society (ARS), New York

Showing no loss of energy or facility, Pablo Picasso was 83 years old when he made this whimsical drawing. Considered a self-portrait, Picasso does not represent the self in the mirror, but the self of the mind, perhaps a younger self or an alter ego who is still potent and sexual. The beard, which he rarely had, harkens to his youth.

Picasso captured this likeness during an intensely productive period. He was newly married to Jacqueline Roque, who was 45 years his junior. It is as if he were defying death with a surge of creativity, looking back on the past through the eyes of the present. And who among us does not have a younger image of ourselves in our mind's eye?

Franz Pourbus the Younger (1569-1622)
Duke of Mantua, ca. 1600
Oil on canvas
32 x 25 inches
Private collection

Flemish artist Frans Pourbus the Younger was one of the most successful portraitists of the early Baroque period. He painted the likenesses of royalty throughout Europe and served as court artist to the Duke of Mantua, Vincenzo I Gonzaga (1562—1612), the subject of this artwork. The Duke was a patron of the arts and sciences who transformed Mantua into a vibrant cultural center. Although his reign was relatively peaceful, Pourbus portrays the Duke in full ceremonial armor, conveying the status due a warrior and statesman.

Auguste Rodin (1840-1917)
Mask of Madame Rodin (Rose Beuret), 1880-82
Bronze
10.375 x 6.875 x 5.875 inches
Private collection

This portrait bust portrays Auguste Rodin's lifelong companion, Rose Beuret; it is one of several heads that he modeled after her. Rodin began living with the young seamstress in 1864 and they conceived a son two years later. Their relationship was a complex one. In addition to being Rodin's lover, Beuret was his housekeeper, studio assistant, and model. Adding to complications were Rodin's public relationships with other women. The two finally married in 1917 when Rodin was 76 and Beuret was 72. She died 16 days later from pneumonia. Rodin passed away 10 months hence and was buried beside her. A large-scale cast of *The Thinker* is erected on their graves.

Roman
Marble bust of a priest
Hadrianic period, AD 117-138
Marble
24.6 x 16.4 x 9.4 inches
Courtesy of The Metropolitan Museum of Art, Private Collection, New York
(L.2007.8.5)

Classical proportion, harmony, and symmetry—the essence of Greek art and thought as defined by Aristotle and Socrates—were upheld as Greek canon. Romans, while often emulating Greek idealism, were more immersed in daily life than the life of the mind practiced by their predecessors. It is in the art of portraiture where the Romans excelled with frankness and a new sense of reality. The most highly valued traits in the Republic included a devotion to public service and military prowess, and citizens sought to project these ideals through their representation in portraiture. This marble bust of a priest, a high government official, is expertly carved; the aquiline nose, thin lips, and sunken cheeks reveal an austere character.
http://www.metmuseum.org/toah/hd/ropo2/hd_ropo2.htm

Daniel Rozin (b. 1961)
Mirror No. 12, 2013
Video camera, custom software, computer, projector, custom projection on wood oval
34 x 60 inches
Courtesy of the artist
and bitforms gallery, NYC

Daniel Rozin creates interactive installations and sculptures that have the unique ability to respond to viewers in real time. *Mirror No. 12* is not an actual

mirror but a video projection that processes live imagery captured by a small camera. Rotating lines are the sole means of representation, resulting in a painterly, albeit digital, image. The torqued projection is bound by an oval frame, evoking the sense of gazing through a peephole—at one's self.

Russian
Saint Nicholas, ca. 1600
12.375 x 11 x 2 inches
Tempera on panel with gold frame
Private collection, Katonah, NY

Icons are typically small religious paintings associated with the Eastern Orthodox (originally Byzantine) Church. Produced in Russia, Greece, Eastern Europe, and the Middle East, icons are believed to bring the worshipper into the presence of those in heaven, acting as "windows" through which the saints can be seen.

Saint Nicholas was a 4th-century Greek bishop who remains the most revered saint in the Russian Orthodox Church. Considered the patron saint of children, Nicholas had a reputation as a secret gift giver, leaving coins in the shoes of the needy, and thus he became a model for the modern-day Santa Claus.

All attributes of an icon are dictated by strict canon laws, which explains the remarkable similarity of facial demeanor, gestural attitude, and attire. As is typical, St. Nicholas is portrayed dressed as a bishop with a golden halo and a white stole embroidered with crosses over each shoulder. His domed forehead, short curly beard, small mouth, and wrinkles (he lived to 73) are also characteristic features.

Jason Salavon (b. 1970)
Portrait (Rembrandt), 2009
Digital C-print
40 x 32.5 inches
Courtesy of the artist and Ronald Feldman Fine Arts, New York

Formerly employed as an artist and programmer in the video game industry, Jason Salavon now writes computer software to create his artwork. For *Portrait (Rembrandt)* Salavon applies a mean-averaging strategy to high-quality reproductions of the Old Master's numerous self-portraits. (Over a 40-year career, Rembrandt produced 75 known self-portraits.) The

result is a ghostly amalgamation; just as quickly as you think you see the artist, he disappears. The eye and mind try desperately to decipher Rembrandt's image, but we are ultimately left with only an ethereal impression.
http://www.rembrandtpainting.net/rembrandt_self_portraits.htm

Lincoln Schatz (b. 1963)
Portrait of Jeff Bezos from the series, *Esquire's Portrait of the 21st Century*, 2008
Generative video work, Mac Mini computer, custom software, display monitor
Courtesy of the artist

In 2008, as part of its 75th anniversary, *Esquire* magazine commissioned new-media artist Lincoln Schatz to create "generative" portraits of the "75 Most Influential People of the 21st Century." Schatz made the individual portraits in his Cube, a ten-foot by ten-foot translucent box fitted with 24 cameras that stream digital video to 24 computers. During each one-hour session, the subjects were encouraged to represent their personalities and interests in whatever ways they desired. Schatz's software program then randomly selects from the thousands of stored video files to present a perpetually evolving progression of overlapping images. The portrait is never the same twice.

In addition to this portrait of Jeff Bezos reading on his Kindle, Schatz's other works include George Clooney dancing with various women, Marc Jacobs doing yoga, LeBron James playing a basketball video game, and Dr. Mehmet Oz operating on a human heart.

Ary Scheffer (1795-1858)
Portrait of René, Cécile, and Louise Franchomme, ca. 1850-51
Oil on canvas
29.75 x 25.625 inches
Richard L. Feigen & Company

Ary Scheffer painted this somber group portrait of Cécile, René, and Louise Franchomme as a gift for their father, who was the artist's neighbor and friend. The children's mother died the year the canvas was completed, which likely accounts for their melancholy expressions.

Scheffer tenderly renders the children's faces, while the cello held by young René is clearly articulated. Their father, Auguste Franchomme, was a celebrated cellist and composer who

often collaborated with Chopin. According to a descendent of the family, the instrument depicted in Scheffer's painting is the celebrated "Duport" cello, which Franchomme purchased at a record price from the famous French cellist Jean-Pierre Duport in 1843. Built in 1711 by Antonio Stradivari, this cello is one of the most famous Stradivarius instruments in existence, and was played by the great 20th-century cellist Mstislav Rostropovich.

Sadly, another tragedy would strike the household when René, at age eighteen, passed away from pneumonia just months after winning first prize in a cello contest at the Paris Conservatoire.

Martin Schoeller (b. 1968)
David Lynch, 1999
Digital chromogenic print
43 x 35 inches
© Martin Schoeller
Courtesy of the artist and Hasted Kraeutler Gallery, NYC

Martin Schoeller's in-your-face approach to portraiture is immediately identifiable. He employs the same hyper-close format, whether photographing President Obama or Angelina Jolie. Here, in David Lynch's piercing blue eyes, viewers may recall the twisted stories from *Twin Peaks*, *Eraserhead,* and *Blue Velvet*. The director's penetrating gaze and his larger-than-life presence are unnerving. Schoeller says, "A photographic close-up is perhaps the purest form of portraiture, creating a confrontation between the viewer and the subject that daily interaction makes impossible, or at least impolite."

Cindy Sherman (b. 1954)
Untitled (MP #473), 2008
Color photograph, Edition 1/6
70.25 x 60 inches
© Cindy Sherman
Courtesy of the artist and Metro Pictures

To create her images, Cindy Sherman assumes the multiple roles of photographer, model, make-up artist, hairdresser, and stylist. She works in series, photographing herself alone in her studio. She conceived her *Society Portraits* in 2008, presenting herself as various socialites who, although fictionalized, seem somehow familiar. Strands of silver hair on this heavily made-up woman divulge the advanced age she is attempting to defy. Her image is alluring and simultaneously pathetic.

Despite her chameleon-like personae, Sherman never considers her work self-portraiture. She says, "These are pictures of emotions personified, entirely of themselves, with their own presence. I'm trying to make other people recognize something of themselves rather than me."
http://www.moma.org/interactives/exhibitions/2012/cindysherman/about-the-exhibition/

Sperandio

Federigo da Montefeltro (1422-1482)
25
Bronze, cast
Diameter 89.5 mm (3.52 inches)
Courtesy of Frances Beatty and Allen Adler

Sperandio, one of the most prolific medallists of the 15th century, depicts Federigo da Montefeltro, the Duke of Urbino, on both sides of this medal. Federigo was a highly successful commander, widely praised for his military ability, his scholarly pursuits, and his benevolent rule. The Duke is shown facing left (as opposed to the right-facing convention for medals), the only way he is ever portrayed, having lost his right eye while jousting. Federigo's nose was also injured in the accident so he subsequently instructed surgeons to remove the bridge. Not only did this give him a distinctive profile, he also claimed it enlarged his field of vision and made him less vulnerable to attack.

Peter Steinhauer (b. 1966)

H'Mong Hoa Minority, Vietnam #96, 2002
Photograph 7/45
22 x 18 inches
Collection of Mona and Ron Schlossberg
© Peter Steinhauer

The H'mong are one of the largest ethnic minorities in Vietnam, with many subgroups. The H'mong Hoa live in northern Vietnam along the Chinese border (hoa is the Vietnamese word for flower). Each minority group has its own traditional style of clothing and head dress; this woman's woven shawl and silver earrings are typical H'mong Hoa attire. (Although not evident in Peter Steinhauer's black-and-white image, the textiles are brightly-colored, thus the designation "flower"). Her hat is made from long strands of her ancestor's hair intertwined with dyed black wool. An American, Steinhauer has lived and photographed in Asia for 20 years. He notes that many Hoa, like this woman, live in remote villages without electricity and have never been photographed. In exchange for permission to take this image, Steinhauer presented the woman with a Polaroid picture of herself.

Florine Stettheimer (1871-1944)

Marcel Duchamp, 1923
Oil on canvas
30 x 26 inches
Private collection of William Kelly Simpson

Florine Stettheimer and her two sisters created a popular salon in their opulent New York City apartment, where they entertained artists, writers, and intellectuals. A frequent visitor, Marcel Duchamp (1887-1968) was one of the most influential artists of the 20th century and Stettheimer painted his likeness several times. This dual portrait shows Duchamp and his alter ego, Rrose Sélavy (a pun on *eros c'est la vie*). The faces are identical, although their hair color differs. As was her custom, Stettheimer includes props that provide psychological insight: the clock refers to Duchamp's life-long interest in time and space as the fourth dimension, the horse reflects his obsession with chess and his identification with the knight, and the entwined American and French flags reference his dual citizenship.

Stettheimer had only one gallery show during her lifetime, where nothing sold. Thereafter she refused to exhibit her work and requested in her will that all her art be destroyed. The family did not comply and two years after her death Stettheimer was featured in a posthumous solo exhibition at the Museum of Modern Art, curated by Duchamp.

Tchambuli Culture (New Guinea, on the Aibom Lake)

Portrait Head, Early 20th century
Wood, pigment, and shell
11.125 x 6.375 x 6.875 inches
1933 Expedition, Dr. Margaret Mead
American Museum of Natural History
(80.0/7377)

The famous American anthropologist Margaret Mead acquired this portrait head during a 1933 expedition to the Sepik River basin of Papua New Guinea. Mead's fieldwork in Melanesia from this period examined the role of gender and how it shaped culture, childrearing, and people's lives. In her influential book, *Sex and Temperament in Three Primitive Societies,* she claimed that females were the dominant sex in the culture of the "Tchambuli" (now spelled Chambri) peoples.

Traditionally these wood carvings were hung outside homes to ward off evil spirits. They depict ancestors, nature spirits, and mythical characters. The question of who this head portrays remains unanswered. Another mystery is whether the portrait is male or female. Either way, it depicts a formidable character whose shell eyes seem to emit fierceness and mysterious power.

Kitagawa Utamaro (1753-1806)

Renowned Beauties Likened to the Six Immortal Poets: Appearing again, the Teahouse Waitress Naniwaya Okita, ca. 1795-6
Woodblock print
14.625 x 9.875 inches
Scholten Japanese Art, New York

Kitagawa Utamaro is one of the great Japanese woodblock artists of the Edo period, which spanned 250 years from the late 1600s to the late 1800s. Utamaro is especially noted for his sensitive and elegant portrayals of women. He created more than 2,000 prints.

The peace and prosperity of the Edo period, when Japan was still closed to the outside world, gave rise to an urban middle class in which the arts flourished. Woodblock prints were among their highest achievement. Called ukiyo-e, "pictures of the floating world," the genre featured landscapes, theater, kabuki, geisha, courtesans, and other pleasurable themes. The prints were mass produced and affordable. Their graphic originality, superb craftsmanship, and flat compositions astounded Europeans who discovered the prints after 1853 when Commander Matthew Perry arrived in Edo (Tokyo) Bay, opening trade with the mysterious island kingdom. The influence of ukiyo-e prints on artists such as Picasso, Matisse, and the Post-Impressionists was immense.

Carl Van Vechten (1880-1964)

Frida Kahlo, March 19, 1932
Photograph
13.50 x 10.50 inches
Hammond Museum permanent collection
Courtesy of the Van Vechten Trust and Yale Collection of American Literature, Beinecke Rare Book and Manuscript Library, Yale University

Carl Van Vechten, a former music and modern dance critic at *The New York Times,* began a new career as a photographer in 1932. Over a span of 40 years, he photographed the most influential cultural figures of his time: artists, writers, actors, dancers, singers, and leaders of the Harlem Renaissance. He took thousands of photographs, printing the black-and-white images himself in the darkroom. Van Vechten's photographs, typically busts or half-length poses, are dramatically staged with an eye to capturing his subject's persona. Van Vechten took several photographs of artists Frida Kahlo and Diego Rivera on March 19, 1932 when the couple was in New York for Rivera's retrospective at the Museum of Modern Art.

Edouard Vuillard (1868-1940)

Self-Portrait with Cane and Straw Hat ca. 1891
Oil on canvas
14.1875 x 11.25 inches
Private collection of William Kelly Simpson
©2013 Artists Rights Society (ARS), New York / ADAPG, Paris

Edouard Vuillard famously remarked, "I don't do portraits. I paint people in their surroundings." Vuillard is best known for his intimate domestic scenes characterized by vivid colors and intense patterning. The shallow picture plane and flat blocks of color in this small self-portrait help to dissolve illusionistic space. This was a radical transformation in style from Vuillard's self-portrait painted two years earlier, which is highly naturalistic in comparison. The change was influenced by the artist's association with the Nabis (the Hebrew word for prophet), a brotherhood of French artists who rebelled against realism and the confines of classicism.
http://www.thejewishmuseum.org/exhibitions/vuillard#sthash.OJq1OLKN.dpuf

Andy Warhol (1928-1987)
Annie Oakley from the *Cowboys and Indians*
series, 1986
Silkscreen TP 27/36
Private collection
©2013 Andy Warhol Foundation for the
Visual Arts/Artist Rights Society (ARS)
New York

Always the iconoclast, Andy Warhol
broke the rule that every print in
an edition should be identical. This
silkscreen of Annie Oakley, part of
a portfolio entitled *Cowboys and
Indians*, is a singular image; no two
prints are exactly the same color, and
sometimes Oakley even faces the
opposite direction.

Oakley (1860-1926) was a star of the
international traveling Buffalo Bill Wild
West Show. Born in rural Ohio, her
father died when she was young and
she helped support her large family
with her amazing shooting ability. She
met her future husband, Frank Butler,
when she was 15, by beating him in a
shooting contest. She once shot the
ash off the cigarette of German Kaiser
Wilhelm II. After the start of WWI,
people quipped that war could have
been avoided had she missed.

Benjamin West (1738-1820)
*Portrait of the Artist's Sons, Raphael West
and Benjamin West Jr., Playing with Dogs*
1775
Oil on canvas
41 x 31.5 inches
Private collection

Neoclassical painter Benjamin West
was the first American artist to
achieve an international reputation.
Born in Pennsylvania, he spent his
entire adult life in England, where he
experienced tremendous success as
both a portraitist and a history painter,
attaining the position of royal court
painter to King George III in 1772.
Living into his 80s, West mentored
three generations of artists and had
a profound influence on painting in
his native country. He welcomed
American artists seeking European
training to his popular London studio.
Among his pupils were John Singleton
Copley, Charles Willson Peale, Gilbert
Stuart, and Thomas Sully.
http://www.getty.edu/art/gettyguide/
artMakerDetails?maker=689

Kehinde Wiley (b. 1977)
Morthyn Brito, 2011
Oil on linen
60 x 50 inches
The Albert Laboz Family Collection
© Kehinde Wiley and Sean Kelly,
New York, New York

Kehinde Wiley paints portraits of
people of color because they are
underrepresented in art history and
because he wants to "see people
who look like me." He selects his
models off the streets of New York
City (and, increasingly, from urban
centers around the world). Rather
than wealthy individuals who can
afford a portrait commission,
Wiley's models are ordinary people
who become the subject of a heroic
painting. They wear their everyday
clothing and often assume poses that
mimic classic European paintings
of noblemen and royalty. Wiley's
backgrounds are purely decorative,
inspired by textiles, wallpaper, and
architectural ornamentation.